Kilpatrick and His Raid

Kilpatrick and His Raid

The Career of a Notable Commander of Union
Cavalry and His Raid through Virginia, 1864
ILLUSTRATED EDITION

James Moore

With Two Short Accounts of the Kilpatrick Raid
by
Joseph G. Vale
&
S. B. Barron

LEONAUR

Kilpatrick and His Raid
The Career of a Notable Commander of Union Cavalry and His Raid through
Virginia, 1864
by James Moore
With Two Short Accounts of the Kilpatrick Raid
by Joseph G. Vale & S. B. Barron

FIRST EDITION

ILLUSTRATED

Leonaur is an imprint of Oakpast Ltd

Copyright in this form © 2017 Oakpast Ltd

ISBN: 978-1-78282-654-5 (hardcover)
ISBN: 978-1-78282-655-2 (softcover)

http://www.leonaur.com

Publisher's Notes

The views expressed in this book are not necessarily
those of the publisher.

Contents

To the
Gallant Officers and Brave Cavalrymen,
Whose Valour and Noble Deeds on the
Different Fields of Glory Have
Entitled Them to the Lasting Gratitude
of Their Country,
the Following Volume
is Respectfully Dedicated,
as a Token of Affectionate Friendship,
By
The Author.

Introduction

The present volume is intended as an historical narrative—chiefly of the cavalry battles in which its subject was engaged; and contains, also, a brief sketch of his previous career. The rebellion itself has called forth more military talent than ever perhaps has been seen at any one period in the annals of the world. The intention of the author is, a plain and unvarnished account of events, in which, with ample materials, considerable personal knowledge, from a service of over three years, and intimate acquaintance with military men, he has studiously endeavoured to render ample justice to everyone, and abide by facts. He believes the work will be interesting, especially to those who have served their country in the field "Three Years or the War!"

CHAPTER 1

Enters West Point a Cadet

In the beautiful Valley of the "Clove," in Northern New Jersey, in the year 1838, Major-General Hugh Judson Kilpatrick, destined to play no inconsiderable role as a cavalry leader, first saw the light. His father was an extensive and enterprising farmer, held in great esteem in the locality; his mother, a lady of good sense and high mental endowments, possessed of the faculty of instilling into the mind of her son those sentiments of honour, truth, and rectitude which form an estimable and a great character.

As the child of their old age, his parents made every effort to afford him those advantages for an education which, at such a period, are so important; his brother and two sisters were already grown up. In person he was, in youth, small, but active, and fond of athletic sports. Providence tenderly watched over his early years, as if designing him to work out some important end in the service of his country. The boy is the man in miniature; so, early he manifested a disposition for a military life, and love of the "bubble reputation." His pulse quickened at the sound of martial music and the gleam of glancing arms.

He might often be found poring over ancient history and accounts of battles, in which he saw Alexander victorious over the immense hosts of Darius; Cyrus, subverting the mighty monarchy of Babylon; Xenophon, with courage, skill, and patience, leading back the Ten Thousand in their famous retreat. He beheld the glory of Athens, Sparta, Corinth, Thebes, and other ancient cities, rendered illustrious by the mighty men who live in ancient story and will never be forgotten. He loved to read about these heroes, and admired their genius, bravery, and good fortune, and was familiar with the names of ancient warriors.

The heroes of Greece were compared, in his young mind, with

11

those of Carthage and Rome, and he dwelt with rapt attention on the deeds of glory that have changed the history of mankind. Thus, the great conquerors of the world and their deeds filled his youthful breast with military ardour, and the fields won, and laurels that decked the brows of heroes, like Alexander, Caesar, Charlemagne, or Napoleon, made him wish for a field on which to emulate their prowess and valour.

It is in the order of Providence that all men are not made alike. One has a bias towards this pursuit, and another towards that; and the very ground on which this young man stood reminded him of the events of the American Revolution, and the efforts made for independence: Washington crossing the frozen Delaware 'mid so many obstacles; his endurance at Valley Forge; his rapid strokes at the enemy on so many occasions; his patriotism, exerted a powerful influence on the mind of the young aspirant for military fame, and were among the first principles that stimulated him to deeds of daring, in their effects beneficial to the country, for which so many have nobly died, that no traitors might mar its union.

In his seventeenth year he took part in public meetings, became immersed in politics, was chosen a delegate to the State Convention, and proved himself one of the first orators in his native State, and indeed was found to possess those gifts to such a degree that, with a mind well cultivated and full of energy, great hopes might be entertained of his usefulness to the nation. Soon after this period, in 1855, having found that his congressional district was entitled to a representative at the Military Academy, he determined to secure the appointment. The person who had the power to grant this was the Hon. George Vail, member of Congress from his district. This gentleman's term in Congress was near expiring, and his friends and party desired and intended to use great efforts for his re-election.

The young subject of this memoir, with many others, was selected to make speeches throughout the district, and he spoke in every town and hamlet, and finally attracted the attention of his member of Congress, who, after the election, which was carried, conferred on Kilpatrick the much coveted appointment.

On the 20th of June, 1856, in his eighteenth year, after the exertion of powers that did great credit to his ability as a popular orator, and showed rare power of eloquence, he made his first entry into the famous Military Academy at West Point as a cadet.

Our plan does not include a description of cadet life, nor of the rigid course of studies and discipline that, for five years, makes the cadet their subject; suffice to remark, from the moment a cadet enters, he is called a "Plebe," when he meets such persecutions and trials as only self-relying, energetic men can withstand. Then it is one long continuous struggle with demerit, studies, and discipline, till the student emerges from the institution a graduate, and, in a degree, a perfect man.

All who possess not these sterling qualities, which have ever characterized great minds, strike, from time to time, the many unseen rocks that render wild and boisterous, the waters upon which the young cadet's boat must ride, and he allows himself to drift into the smoother waters of a citizen's life. Kilpatrick entered on his studies with zest, and applied himself diligently to master the grand principles that form the soldier. That he was well prepared to enter the institution, we are reliably informed. In mathematical science, engineering, ethics, and other branches, it is certain he had, on leaving, an excellent knowledge, and, most likely, on other subjects equally proficient. The class numbered one hundred and four; of these, fifty graduated, and he the fifteenth in that number.

The delivery of the valedictory was an honour which was conferred upon him. It is an oration of good style, noble sentiments, full of eloquent passages and patriotic motives, and reflects great credit on the author. We may, on a future page, have occasion to furnish the reader with a few extracts.

The address was delivered before a select company of officers of the army, and the beauty and fashion of North and South which thronged the graceful little chapel on the occasion—was listened to with great attention, and produced a profound impression, and one not soon to be forgotten.

One incident, during his stay at the academy, must not be omitted, as it illustrates fully the principle of action and manly daring of the subject of this memoir. He had been promoted to the rank of Cadet Officer, for soldierly bearing, and, in the exercise of his duties was interfered with by one of the cadets, who made a disturbance, and, relying on his strength, answered only in an insolent manner when reproved—promising, if reported, that he would thrash Kilpatrick. The latter performed his duty, reported him, was attacked, and though but a small man, and the other one of the largest in the academy, planted his blows with such activity, vigour, and skill, that, at the end of forty minutes, victory declared in his favour, and the discomfited foe was soon after court-martialled and dismissed from the the service.

Thus, we see that he fearlessly performed his duty, and was not to be driven from it by bullying. This contest manifested the undeveloped physical and mental resources he possessed, and warned others that it was a hazardous experiment to tamper with him. Though great good-will always existed between him and his companions; and that he had a heart formed for friendship one can see from the valedictory itself, which feelingly alludes to the pleasant times they spent together. He graduated at that important period when the corrupt political gamblers of the South, who, for years, had been cherishing treason next their hearts while swearing fealty to the Union, had, at last goaded themselves on to fire a hostile shot at the Stars and Stripes, long venerated and loved by a free nation.

Kilpatrick was sitting in his room when this news reached the Point, creating the liveliest sensation. In common with every loyal patriot, his heart swelled with indignation, and he longed to graduate, that he might go at once into the field, and meet the enemies of the Union. It was now but April, and the class was to graduate in June; the intervening time till then seemed an age; he wanted to be off at once, to join those already in the field. When the mind is filled with an important design, or a great idea, whether love or war, politics or religion, it is likely that such design, or idea, will be communicated, and influence others. Some there sided with the South.

It was a critical moment, for, at the commencement of the rebellion, the Union could send out men and raise money; but it was not so easy to get efficient officers. The influence of this young man, ardent, patriotic, and eloquent, was of great benefit to the country; inasmuch as by it a request was made, on the part of thirty-seven of the class out of fifty, to be permitted to graduate at once, and take the field.

Kilpatrick and his friend and classmate, the late lamented Colonel Kingsbury, who afterwards fell at Antietam, and Beaumont, a roommate, drew up this petition, addressed to the President, and sent it to Washington. The request was granted and the class graduated. It was a great day at West Point. The acquaintances of the young men were there, proud to see their success, and happy too.

The eloquent words of the valedictory died away in the beautiful little chapel, and the attentive and gratified audience had dissolved, some one way, some another; but there was one, the loveliest of her sex, who, more than any other, hung upon the lips of the young orator, and drank in the words of that address with thrilling pride and

14

gratification.

Nor can it be imagined that a sympathetic glow failed to animate the breast of the speaker on that occasion, or that his keen blue eye and quickening pulse, and features radiant with happiness as well as with pride, had not felt sensible of her presence. For already they were betrothed; the day fixed, a remote one in August, was to see them united in holy bonds. Of all suitors for her hand, the orator of the day was the favoured one who was to bear away the treasure of a lovely woman's devoted affections, whose sweetness of disposition, good sense, and mental accomplishments, were equal to her personal attractions.

Reader! there is a beautiful banner hanging at the headquarters of one, who on that day was united in the chapel before mentioned, at West Point, to her whose hands made it; and her name, the sweet name of Alice, is inscribed on its streamer, and often has waved in danger and in victory. The youthful couple were standing together at the hotel, when a classmate remarked: "Kill, is going to the field, and may not return. Better get married now." The advice was taken; the chaplain was at hand—admiring friends around; the mystic knot was tied, and the happy pair started for Washington that evening, with the prayers of all for their welfare.

Thus, Providence smiled on the path of this youth who had entered West Point, graduated, and married. The boy had become the man. Studies, and discipline, and theories, were now about to be put into practice. He had entered the arena, and was about to grapple with the responsibilities and stern realities of life. "None but the brave deserve the fair," and a brave spirit he had, whose impatience soon led him into the tented field. His wisdom in marrying soon became apparent, for scarce had the honeymoon ended when, in the first charge, in the first battle of the war, on the memorable 11th of June, 1861, he fell wounded on the field, at the head of Duryea's Zouaves, at Big Bethel. To a wounded man a good nurse is as needful, almost, as a surgeon, and what nurse equals a loving wife?

He had been serving at Fortress Monroe with Duryea's Zouaves, with General Benj. F. Butler. Several reconnoissances had been made that convinced the commanding general of the enemy being in force at Big Bethel, between Fortress Monroe and Yorktown. It was determined to attack this force by moving upon the main road to Yorktown, while General Butler, in person, would make an attack, by water, on Yorktown, cutting off the retreat of the rebels. General Pierce, with from three to four thousand men, moved on Big Bethel from two points—Newport News and Fortress Monroe.

The young officer, about to make his first debut as a warrior, was put in command of a part of Duryea's Zouaves, and led the advance. Having made a rapid movement in the direction of Yorktown, he surprised and captured the enemy's picket-post, one mile from Big Bethel, and, marching all night, arrived in sight of the enemy's works in the morning. He was directed to make a reconnaissance, which ended in a general engagement. He moved his men across an open field, and, though never before under fire, they moved with the steadiness of veterans. The enemy was driven out of his works, and took up a position behind a creek. Many brave men were killed and wounded, and this young officer, leading his troops gallantly on, was wounded in the right thigh with a grape-shot; notwithstanding this wound, though drenched in blood, and suffering great pain, he led his troops in several subsequent charges, till loss of blood forced him to retire, and he was borne off from this his first field.

Thus, struggled he, and thus struggled, too, the gallant Greble, a young lieutenant of great promise, of Kilpatrick's own regiment, the First United States Artillery, who, in charge of the artillery, fell with many brave men in this battle, admired by all who knew him, and universally lamented.

Though our troops, after having made many charges, were, through mismanagement, forced to retire from the field, yet the valour of officers and men aroused the bravery of the nation.

Kilpatrick, having returned to New York city to recover from his wound, did not return to the field before September, when we find him at Washington, promoted to the rank of lieutenant-colonel, preparing his regiment, the Harris Light Cavalry, for the field. He was also promoted to First Lieutenant First Artillery in the regular army. He soon won the respect of his superiors, was one of an Examining Board for examining cavalry officers of the volunteer service, and had, besides other duties, that of Inspector-General of McDowell's Division. When, on March 8th, 1862, the grand army of the Potomac marched on Manassas, Kilpatrick's regiment having the advance, he left Arlington at daylight, and drove the rear guard of the retreating army of Lee from the burning ruins of Manassas. At seven o'clock, p.m., of the same day, having marched thirty miles, he was twelve miles in advance of the grand army.

The following day, he advanced to Catlett's Station, and there re-

Battle of Big Bethel and death of Lieutenant Greble

mained till the middle of April, when McDowell's column moved on Falmouth, when he again was in the advance. Meantime the grand army of the Potomac had moved to Alexandria, thence to Fortress Monroe, and was already thundering at the gates of Richmond. Kilpatrick moved down the road to Falmouth, met and routed Lee's cavalry and infantry, five miles from that place. At one o'clock the following morning, with Colonel Bayard, and the First Pennsylvania Cavalry, he rode over the rebel barricades, and entered, at daylight, the town of Falmouth. For this daring ride, in which many gallant men fell, and made both regiments famous. Bayard was made a general, and Kilpatrick was complimented and thanked in orders by the commanding general.

General Pope now assumed command of the army of Virginia, and Kilpatrick was afforded an opportunity of making one of those series of raids for which he afterwards became so well known.

The main body of Lee's army was then concentrated at Richmond, but the famous Stonewall Jackson was at Gordonsville, and in the Shenandoah Valley. His principal line of communication and supplies was by the Virginia Central Railroad, running from Gordonsville to Richmond.

Kilpatrick was ordered to strike this railroad at different points, and break up Jackson's communication with Richmond. He made one raid after another, striking it at Beaver Dam, Frederick Hall, and Hanover Junction, burning stations and destroying the track, in spite of every effort on the part of the enemy to prevent it. Though he attacked him at different times, he either whipped him or made good his own escape.

His services were acknowledged by General Pope, in an official communication and by telegraph, and the whole country exulted in the successes of the young officer who dared thus boldly to operate upon the enemy's communications, at so great a distance, and in his own country. This was accomplished in July and August, 1862.

In August, General Pope concentrated his forces at Culpepper, and next day was fought the memorable battle of Cedar Mountain, an engagement in which the cavalry took no important part, but watched the flanks,

Kilpatrick was picketing the Rapidan, and was the first to give the alarm that the whole rebel army under Lee had left the defences of Richmond, and was marching to annihilate Pope's army at Culpepper. When the truth of this was ascertained, General Pope determined to fall back on Centreville heights. In this retrograde movement, Kilpatrick's regiment was with General Bayard's cavalry brigade that covered the rear of our army till it reached the defences about Washington.

The memorable events of these days are still fresh in the minds of the people. Everyone knows the part taken by Kilpatrick and his regiment in the battles of Brandy Station, Sulphur Springs, Freedman's Ford, Waterloo Bridge, Groveton, Haymarket, and, finally, the disastrous Battle of Bull Bun, and the subsequent efforts made by this young officer to protect our disorganised columns, as they fell back on Washington. Though his regiment had dwindled down from 700 men to less than 350, yet, when General Bayard made a call for men, when the rebel Fitzhugh Lee dashed on our tired and worn-out troops, at Fall's Church, it was one of the few to respond to the call.

Bayard's cavalry remained south of Washington, and did not participate in the glorious victories of Antietam and South Mountain, which followed in quick succession, and wiped out, in rebel blood, the disgrace cast upon our arms through the stupendous military blunder and defeat of Bull Run.

But neither was Bayard nor Kilpatrick idle, A want of some proper organisation, and especially of concentration, in the cavalry, had long been felt by those who believed in the utility of this arm of the service.

Every effort was made, by different cavalry officers, and especially by Bayard, the then great cavalry chief of the Army of the Potomac, to effect some permanent and beneficial change. Major-General Burnside, then in command, allowed many valuable changes to be made. But it was not till General Hooker assumed command of the army, that the cavalry regiments scattered throughout the army were gathered together and massed as a distinct arm of the service.

General Hooter believed in cavalry, and brigades and divisions were now formed and organised, and finally the Cavalry Corps of the Army of the Potomac was organised, and Stoneman placed at its head.

The rebel cavalry under Stuart, Fitzhugh Lee, and Hampton, had long been organised into a formidable body; and this organisation necessitated a corresponding one in the Federal cavalry. The Southern chivalry, it was plain to be seen, in no small degree relied upon and were proud of their cavalry. That the men of the North could be taught to ride, and, especially, meet in saddle, in fierce combat, the cavaliers of the South, was derided by the proud and insolent rebels, who looked upon the independence of the Confederacy as a foregone conclusion.

How much they reckoned without their host was soon made apparent.

Stuart had massed, at Culpepper, his corps, consisting of a formidable body of men, not less than fifteen thousand cavalry and twenty pieces of artillery.

That this force was to be met—that a cavalry battle must ensue—on the first movement of the grand armies of Lee and Hooker, was well known to the army; but more especially to those more intimately concerned—Stoneman and his men. Consequently, no pains were spared, schools of instruction were established, boards of examination organised, old and incompetent officers dismissed, and intelligent, young, and daring men placed at the heads of regiments and brigades. Every effort was made to secure success in the struggle so near at hand.

General Averill, with his division, crossed the Rappahannock at Kelly's Ford, about the middle of March (1863), and engaged the enemy's cavalry, a few miles beyond, with great success.

This was most encouraging to the entire corps, but was only an ante-past of the great victory over Stuart and his men, on the broad plains of Brandy Station, a few days later.

The time had now arrived for the spring campaign. Contending armies were about to meet in hostile array on the plains of Chancellorsville, and a great battle was imminent. Mighty forces, on each side, were meeting for the strife. Corps of infantry and heavy guns were being forwarded to the scene of action, and the cavalry was to act no unimportant part. It was decided that Stoneman should cross the Rappahannock and the Rapidan, and fasten upon the communications of the enemy, destroy bridges and railroads, and prevent a retreat of the enemy should he be defeated, as was fully expected.

The cavalry corps consisted of three divisions, commanded by Generals Pleasanton, Averill, and Gregg, and the regular brigade under Buford.

Leaving General Pleasanton to co-operate directly with the main army, Stoneman left his encampment and marched for the Rappahannock, intending to cross at Beverly Ford, and dispose of the rebel cavalry gathered there under Stuart, before moving to the rear of Lee's army.

High water and bad roads, however, baffled all attempts to cross for several days, and finally this plan was abandoned. Stoneman, however, not discouraged, moved rapidly to Kelly's Ford, a few miles lower down, and moved his entire force boldly between the rebel cavalry and the main army under Lee, to and across, the Rapidan, and pushed rapidly on, striking the Virginia Central, far in the rear of Lee's army, at Louisa Court-House.

From this point, Stoneman moved forward, crossed the North Anna, and halted at the point on the main Richmond road where the road from Spottsylvania to Goochland Court-House intersected it. Kilpatrick, then commanding a brigade of Gregg's division, was ordered to cover the rear, and hold in check any forces of Stuart that might be inclined to follow.

After dark, he silently left his camp, making a rapid night march, and joined General Stoneman. From information received by stragglers and contrabands from Lee's army, there was every reason to believe that general had been defeated, and was now retreating towards Richmond. The time for Stoneman to act had now arrived.

Accordingly, with coolness and promptitude, he issued his orders: Gregg was sent to destroy the bridges over the North Anna, and interrupt communication in that direction; Colonel Davis was sent to destroy the bridges over the South Anna, south of the Fredericksburg railroad; Colonel Windham, with details from regiments of his brigade, was sent to destroy the canal along the James River; and finally, Kilpatrick, with the Harris Light Cavalry, was sent to burn the railroad and meadow bridges on the Chickahominy, five miles from the city of Richmond. Meanwhile, Stoneman, with the main force, remained to cover those movements, in case Stuart should make his appearance.

It is not the intention of the author to follow out the details of these operations. Gregg was very successful; Windham partially so; Davis, after fulfilling his orders, joined Kilpatrick at Gloucester Point, upon whom devolved the most difficult and dangerous as well as the most important task. From its great success, and on account of forming the most important feature in Stoneman's great raid—though anxious to hurry on to the description of the great cavalry battles which followed three months later—the occasion demands a narrative of the principal events that covered Kilpatrick and his men with glory, and made the name of this gallant young officer resonant from every tongue.

With his own regiment, the Harris Light, numbering four hundred and forty-seven men, and with such subordinate officers as Davis, McIrvin, Grinton, Cook, Mitchell, Estis, and Hackley, he parted with Stoneman and his cavalry, in the earliest hours of an April day, and, full of high hopes, started on his perilous expedition.

Advancing rapidly, without cessation, he encamped at night thirteen miles from the rebel capital. He pushed boldly forward, though surrounded by the enemy, and, as was ascertained from scouts, every road was swarming with their troops.

Avoiding too formidable bodies, and driving before him the smaller forces that dared oppose his march, he struck the Fredericksburg railroad at day-dawn nine miles from Richmond.

He then crossed over, and moved down the Brook Pike within two miles of the city, into which he drove, in confusion, a section of artillery and a considerable force of infantry and cavalry.

An *aide-de-camp* of General Winder, by name Captain Brown, and fourteen men, his escort, were captured and paroled, Kilpatrick dating the parole from the city of Richmond.

The *aide-de-camp*, an intelligent young man, was perfectly astonished at the bold daring of the "Yankee raider," remarking, "You're mighty daring sort of fellows; but you will certainly be captured before sundown!"

"That may all be," said Kilpatrick, "but we intend to do a mighty deal of mischief first;" a prediction amply verified in a few days.

He left a portion of his troops to engage the rebel batteries, which were visible at no great distance, and, guided by a negro, moved through a plantation, and, unobserved by the enemy, burned the railroad bridge over the Chickahominy. The troops were led in safety across, and the grand object of the expedition was fully attained, though in the face of rebel batteries that had a complete range of the important bridges laid in ashes by this intrepid commander.

The situation was now imminently perilous. Rebel columns could be seen moving up the Brook Pike, and up the road to Mechanicsville, to intercept and capture this little band of heroes, and all hopes of returning to Stoneman were rendered impossible.

The leader glanced at his map, and, for one moment only, an anxious expression clouded his features, but vanished as it came. He sprang to his feet, shouting: "To horse, men! we are all right; we are all safe yet!"

Placed at their head, he urged rapidly onwards across a field to the house of a planter; and, finding a negro, who satisfactorily answered his questions, and knew the locality well, he mounted him on horseback, and under his guidance struck the main road from Richmond, and in less than two hours arrived at Hanover Town, on the banks of the Pamunkey.

Crossing on flatboats, he destroyed all the boats and bridges for miles above and below, thus rendering every attempt at successful pursuit unavailing.

Cheer after cheer now rent the air, and the skilful manner in which their leader conducted the hazardous enterprise, strewn with one difficulty after another, now happily surmounted, and the impassable barrier of a broad, deep, and rapid stream being interposed, and pursuit impossible, gave him such a hold on the hearts of his men, and such a feeling of confidence in him was inspired, as to raise their enthusiasm to the highest point of admiration, which was susceptible of no diminution, but rose higher and higher.

You, who have led soldiers on the battlefield, through perils, carnage, and death-—who, successful, the danger past, can enter into the feelings of these brave men, and understand the peculiar faculty this leader possesses of inspiring his men with confidence, respect, and love, and that to a degree seldom equalled.

The expedition did not end with the accomplishment of its grand design; but rebel stores, trains of wagons, one after another were destroyed, and Aylett's Station, with its immense supplies for the rebel army, was laid in ashes. All along the road, between King's and Queen's Court-House, everything that could be of use to the enemy met the same fate; and at last the Federal lines were reached at Gloucester Point.

Having rested a few days, Kilpatrick, with his own regiment and the Eighth Illinois Cavalry, comprising, in all, about a thousand men, marched through Gloucester Court-House and Dragon's Swamp, and thence to Urbana, on the Rappahannock.

The troops crossed in transports sent for the purpose, and were conducted up the Peninsula, rejoining General Hooker at Falmouth, after describing a complete circle of the entire rebel army. The loss in killed, wounded, and missing, in this daring expedition, amounted to forty-nine men in all.

It was completed in five days, during which sixty miles a day were traversed, and the wearied men and horses then obtained a brief repose.

Here we will leave them for the present, while the gallant leader, whose star was in the ascendant, rests upon his laurels, and make ready for the great events which follow closely upon these.

CHAPTER 2

Bravery and Gallant Deeds of Kilpatrick

Hooker had now, once more, gathered his army about him, and the depressing results of his failure at Chancellorsville were obviated and lost sight of in the great interest felt for his next movements.

Positive information had been received that the rebel chief was breaking up his camp, and had put his various columns in motion; tall spirals of smoke were seen rising above the high tree-tops and from among the rugged hills around Fredericksburg. Heavy clouds of dust had been rising for hours, and were seen rolling on towards Culpepper, indicating a vast movement of men in that direction.

Hooker did not hesitate for one moment. He knew, full well, the meaning of these military signs, and the course he should pursue.

A reconnaissance in force was made across the Rappahannock, to remove all doubts, while with his main army, he marched for Catlett's Station. Information reached him here, that Stuart had been massing his cavalry near Beverly Ford, for an intended raid into Maryland and Pennsylvania. This must be prevented, and the real object of Lee discovered. General Pleasanton, the then cavalry chief, was directed to move, with his entire command, and attack and defeat Stuart, thus nipping in the bud the anticipated raid, and discovering at the same time the position of the rebel army.

On the morning of the 9th of May, the various cavalry columns took up their line of march in obedience to the orders of Pleasanton, who, thoroughly acquainted with and master of his subject, had well matured his plans for the first as well as greatest cavalry battle ever fought on this continent.

Many of my readers have visited, at some time, our army while

24

encamped on the banks of the Rappahannock, and well remember the broad, open plains extending far back from this romantic river, in the direction of Stevensburg, Culpepper, and the battlefield of Cedar Mountain. Here Stuart had massed his men—here the great cavalry battle occurred—and here the mouldering bones of many a cavalry hero attest full well how that field was fought and won.

Gregg, with two divisions, crossed at early dawn the Rappahannock, at Beverly Ford, intending to push boldly out well in the direction of Stevensburg, and then move upon the enemy's flank and rear at Brandy Station. Pleasanton, with Buford and the gallant Colonel Davis, crossed at Beverly Ford, surprised the enemy in his camp, and had crossed his entire force before he was aware of the movement. A desperate battle now ensued. Davis fell in the very centre of the enemy's camps, leading a gallant charge; young Parsons, of his staff, leaped his horse over the prostrate body of his chief, and killed, at one blow, the author of his death; the enemy was steadily pressed back, foot by foot, until he had been driven upwards of two miles.

It would have fared ill with our cavalry, at this point, had it not been for the timely arrival of General Ames, with his brigade of veteran infantry. These were pushed well in, and fought side by side with our cavalry throughout the day.

At 10.30 a.m. Gregg came in sight of the plain about Brandy Station. It was indeed a glorious spectacle. The whole battlefield was before him. Far to the left the artillery, from the low bills, was sending shot and shell through and through the rushing squadrons; and the bright gleam of sabres flashing in the sunlight could be distinctly seen, while the wild shout of friend and foe rushing to the charge was borne to the ears of those men of Gregg, who now, for the first time, saw the dust and smoke of battle, and longed to mingle in the fray.

The word was given—their willing blades leaped from their scabbards, and with one wild, exultant shout they dashed across the field, on, over the railroad, and, with Windham at their head, actually rode over and through the headquarters of Stuart, the rebel chief

Here they were met by rebel columns too powerful to withstand. Nobly fought the First New Jersey; and, like brave men too, fought the First Pennsylvania. But all in vain! Back they rolled, before the formidable host, down the lull, and, despite the mighty efforts made, it seemed as if all were lost At this critical moment Kilpatrick's battle-flag floated out upon the field, and after it came the disciplined squadrons of the Harris Lights the Tenth New York, and the First Maine. In

Young Parsons avenging the death of Colonel Davis, at the Battle of Beverley Ford

echelons of squadrons, by regiments, he quickly formed his brigade, and down rushed upon the rebel cavalry, swarming on the plain below. The Tenth New York met and recoiled before the shock. Back also was borne the Harris Light. At the repulse of his own proud regiment, Kilpatrick was wild with excitement.

The First Maine had not yet been engaged, and was slowly moving down. Kilpatrick dashed to the head of this regiment, shouting, "Men of Maine! you must save the day! Follow me!"

In one solid mass this splendid raiment circled first to the right, and then moving in a straight line at a run struck the rebel columns in flank. The shock was terrific! Down went the rebels before this wild rush of maddened horses, biting sabres, and whistling balls.

On rode the men of Maine, and as they passed the Harris Light and Tenth New York now relieved from the attack in front, Kilpatrick's voice rang loud and clear above the noise and din of battle.

"Back the Harris Light! Back the Tenth New York! Reform your squadrons and charge!" The hill was won: Windham's guns, lost in the first charge, recaptured, and the day was saved; the enemy gave way before Gregg's repeated charges, and, at four o'clock p. m. he made a junction with the cavalry under Pleasanton.

The victory was fairly won, and, had one of our divisions under Duffie come upon the field at the time ordered, it might have been decisive. The enemy's infantry could now be seen marching down from Culpepper, to the relief of their worn-out and defeated cavalry. The object of the attack was accomplished: Stuart's raid prevented, and the important information gained that Lee was marching for Maryland. Pleasanton withdrew his victorious squadrons in safety across the Rappahannock, and thus ended a day replete with glory to our arms.

Our cavalry had met the enemy in superior force, in fair combat, on the open ground, and the boasted chivalry, the cavaliers of the South, had been ridden down, and vanquished by the men of the North. The following day Pleasanton was made a Major-General, and Kilpatrick a Brigadier. These splendid cavalry battles, as we have already remarked, exposed the real movements of Lee, and had convinced Hooker, beyond a doubt, that it was his opponent's intention to march for the Potomac, at some point near or above Harper's Ferry.

Hooker made no attempt whatever, to prevent or check this advance; but contented himself with moving slowly on, and carefully watching the movements of the rebel army, till his various corps reached Fairfax Court-House. Here he made his headquarters for sev-

Kilpatrick at Brandy Station

eral days, pushing his columns well out in the direction of Aldie and Thoroughfare Gap. This delay was purposely made, that Lee might have ample time to reach a point from which he could not retreat without a battle. But as Lee did not make his appearance on the banks of the Potomac as quickly as anticipated, some uneasiness was created in the mind of Hooker. A question arose, where was the rebel army? and what were the intentions of Lee?

This it was necessary should be ascertained, and the question could alone be solved by an armed reconnoissance.

Pleasanton had already moved His command to Manassas and Bull Run, and it now devolved on him to make this reconnoissance and gain the required information.

Accordingly, he moved at early dawn, on the morning of the 18th of June, crossed the plains of Manassas, passed the celebrated battlefield of Groveton, and by noon came in sight of the high hills about Aldie.

General Kilpatrick was now sent in the advance with his brigade, consisting of the Harris Light. Colonel Davies; Fourth New York, Colonel Cesnola; the First Massachusetts; First Rhode Island; Sixth Ohio Cavalry, Colonel Duffie; and a section of artillery, under Lieutenant Randall.

Kilpatrick was directed to move through Aldie; thence to and through Ashby's Gap, ascertain the enemy's movements, and rejoin the cavalry corps at Nolan's Ferry on the Potomac. Colonel Duffie, with his regiment, the First Rhode Island cavalry, was directed to move through Thoroughfare Gap and join Kilpatrick in the valley beyond.

Scarcely had his advance reached the town of Aldie, when it came directly upon the advance guard of Fitzhugh Lee. This was entirely unexpected. No enemy was supposed to be on the Aldie side of Bull Run mountains.

The general rode to the front, ran his eye over the field for a moment, and then rapidly gave his orders. He had taken in the whole field at one rapid glance, and saw the important points that must be gained. The Harris Light Cavalry was directed to charge straight down the road, through the town, gain and hold the long, low hill over which ran the road from Middleburg. With anxious eye, he watched the charge on which so much depended, saw that it was successful, and quickly and resolutely pushed in one regiment after another on the right of the Harris Light, till the high hills, far on the right of Aldie, were gained.

This fine disposition was made, and important position won, before the rebel general Fitzhugh Lee could make a single effort to prevent it, although he had a division of cavalry at his buck.

He soon recovered, however, from the temporary surprise, and for two hours made most desperate efforts to regain the position lost. He struck the right, left, and centre, in quick succession, while his battery of Blakely guns thundered forth their messengers of death.

But all in vain! Kilpatrick's gallant men—the heroes of Brandy Station—met and hurled back each charge, while Randall's battery, ignoring entirely the rebel guns, sent his canister and shells tearing through the heavy columns of the enemy.

On this day, Kilpatrick did wonders. He fought under the eye of his chief, and where bullets flew the thickest and where the shock came the heaviest, there rang his cheering voice and there flashed his sabre. His own regiment, the Harris Light, had failed to meet his hopes on the plains of Brandy Station. This was known to the officers of that splendid organisation, and on that very morning they had petitioned their general for an opportunity to retrieve their reputation. The opportunity was at hand.

A large force of the enemy occupied a strong position, behind rail barricades encircling large stacks of hay. For a long time, rebel sharpshooters, from this secure position, had baffled every attempt to advance our lines on the left. The general ordered up a battalion of the Harris Light. Quickly it came! Addressing a few encouraging words to the men, and then turning to Major Irvin, the officer in command, he said, pointing to the barricades: "Major! *there* is the opportunity you have asked for. Go! take *that position!*" Away dashed this officer and his men. In a moment the enemy was reached, and the struggle begun. The horses could not leap the barricade, but the men dismounted, scaled those formidable barriers, and, with drawn sabres, rushed upon the hidden foe, who quickly asked for quarter.

Another incident occurred worth mentioning. Colonel Cesnola, of the Fourth New York Cavalry, had that morning, through mistake, been placed under arrest, and, his sword being taken from him, was without arms. But in one of these wild charges, made early in the morning, his regiment hesitated. Forgetting that he was under arrest and without command, he flew to the head of his regiment, reassured his men, and, without a weapon to give or ward a blow, led them to the charge. This gallant act was seen by his general, who, meeting him on his return, said: "Colonel, you are a brave man; you are released from arrest;" and, taking his own sword from his side, handed it to the colonel, saying: "Here is my sword;" wear it in honour of this day!" In the next charge, Colonel Cesnola fell, desperately wounded, and was taken prisoner.

The rebel general, being foiled at every point, resolved to make one more desperate effort. Silently and quickly he amassed a heavy force upon our extreme right, and, led by General Rosser, made one of the most desperate and determined charges of the day. Kilpatrick was aware of this movement, and, satisfied that his men, exhausted as they were, could not withstand the charge, had already sent for re-enforcements.

Before these could reach him, the shock came.

The First Massachusetts had the right, and fought as only brave men could to stem the tide that steadily bore them back, until the whole right gave way. Back rushed our men in wild confusion, and on came the victorious rebel horsemen. The general saw, with anguish, his flying soldiers, yet, in this extremity, retained his presence of mind, and proved himself worthy the star he had won at Brandy Station.

Sending orders for the centre and left to stand fast, and for Randall not to move, but double-shot his guns, he placed himself at the head of the First Maine, sent to his assistance, and coolly waited till the rebel charging columns had advanced within fifty yards of Randall's guns. He then shouted "*Forward!*" and the same regiment that saved the day at Brandy Station was destined to save the day at Aldie. Rosser's men could not withstand the charge, but broke and fled up the hill. The general's horse was killed in the charge, and here the brave Colonel Doughty fell.

The general determined now to complete the victory, and, mounting a fresh horse, he urged on the First Maine and First Massachusetts, sent orders for his whole line to advance, and then sounded the charge. Lee struggled for a few minutes against this advance, and then ordered a retreat, which ended in a rout. His troops were driven in confusion as far as Middleburg, and night alone saved the remnant of his command.

This was by far the most bloody cavalry battle of the war. The rebel chivalry had again been beaten, and Kilpatrick, who was the only general on the field, at once took a proud stand among the most famous of our Union cavalry generals. The fame of our cavalry was now much enhanced, and caused the greatest joy to the nation.

Well-founded expectations, from the success of our arms, gave the hope of bringing the war to a close at no distant day. The arm of the

GENERAL KILPATRICK PRESENTING HIS OWN SWORD TO COLONEL CESNOLA

service that had achieved such victories became an object of pride to the people. We now had a cavalry force and cavalry leaders able to cope with the chivalry. The rapid movements of Jugurtha and the Numidian Cavalry had been surpassed by the Richmond raid, already described. The dash of "Light Horse Harry Lee" of the Revolution, and the celebrated chaise of the Six Hundred, were equalled.

Charged by shot and shell,
Boldly they rode and well,
Into the jaws of death,
Into the mouth of hell.
Rode the Six Hundred.

The skilful combination and rapid execution which the reader has not failed to observe as some of the characteristics of the young general, were among the causes of his working out so many problems of difficult solution. Nature and education seem to have endowed him with that quickness of perception, readiness of mind, and strength of purpose, which, when the will determines, no impediment is sufficient to deter from putting into successful execution what a rapid glance suffices to comprehend. To those of our readers who have not seen General Kilpatrick, a personal description may not be uninteresting, in connection with this relation of events in which he is so naturally conspicuous.

His stature is five feet seven inches; average weight one hundred and forty pounds; physical organisation such as to combine agility, gracefulness, and ease of movement, with strength, endurance, and energy; temperament nervous and restless, but sanguine, taking views from nature in her smiling mood; hopeful, always calculating on success; his face in all its outlines is well delineated, oval in form, complexion fair, teeth regular and white, nose prominent, eyes blue and piercing upon occasion, expression frank, free, open, and cordial; manners easy, blending dignity with accessibility, and rendering respect always where it is due—and this is one cause of much popularity. The greatest characters are usually the most easy of access, and good breeding greatly consists in putting everyone at ease. With these qualities, a certain eloquence, colloquial and extemporaneous, distinguishes the subject of this memoir.

After the Battle of Aldie, Pleasanton determined to push on through Middleburg to Ashby's Gap, and, if possible, force Stuart back on the rebel infantry. Colonel Craig, the following morning, made a reconnaissance to Middleburg, and, after a slight skirmish, occupied the town. June 2lst, Pleasanton advanced with his entire corps; Buford held the right, and Gregg the left.

The enemy was met a short distance beyond Middleburg, and forced steadily back to Upperville. Here the enemy made a determined stand. This he found was absolutely necessary, as otherwise the force in front of Buford, who was on a road far to the rights would be unable to reach Ashby's Gap, and, consequently, would be cut off and captured. Pleasanton saw the necessity of at once routing the force in front of Gregg; and, accordingly, Kilpatrick was ordered to charge the town. This was done most handsomely, sabres alone being used—a weapon this general always had great confidence in, and by its use now drove the enemy from the town precipitately, through Ashby's Gap and back on Lee's infantry.

While the fight was going on, scouts from Buford's column had crossed the mountain, and discovered that the advance of Lee's army, under Longstreet, was moving up the valley towards Williamsport, on the Potomac. The following day Pleasanton moved slowly back to Aldie, and thence to Harper's Ferry—crossed the river, and with the main army, under Hooker, moved to Frederick City. Here many important changes of the army took place. General Hooker was relieved from command of the Army of the Potomac, and Major-General Meade placed at its head.

Major-General Stahl, commanding a division of cavalry numbering upwards of five thousand men, was relieved, and General Kilpatrick placed in command. Captain Merritt, of the regulars, was promoted to the rank of brigadier, and assumed command of the Regular Cavalry Brigade. Captains Custer and Farnsworth, of Pleasanton's staff, had been promoted to the rank of brigadier-general, and assigned to command brigades under General Kilpatrick. The cavalry corps now consisted of three large divisions, commanded by Buford, Gregg and Kilpatrick This brings us up to the commencement of those great strategic movements which forced the enemy, who had now crossed the State of Maryland and reached with his advance the banks of the Susquehanna, to give us battle on the glorious field of Gettysburg. An account of this battle, and especially the part taken in it by the cavalry, will be described in the following chapter.

CHAPTER 3

Little Round Top

Before entering on the details of this battle, the reader's attention is invited to a retrospective view of the events that had intervened since the disastrous day that saw a Union Army panic-stricken, and fleeing before astonished traitors in arms against their country, on the bloody field of Bull Run, in which a disgrace so great had this advantage to the nation: it entirely removed the public contempt, almost universally entertained hitherto, regarding the magnitude of the rebellion.

We have seen the subject of this memoir, on that eventful day, doing what he could to preserve our shattered forces, as they fell back on the defences of Washington and filled the dismayed inhabitants with terror. He also was present, when, at Baltimore, a mob endeavoured to stop the trains for Washington, and exhibited there that bold intrepidity which marks his character.

The nation will ever remember with gratitude the brave men who at that period defied the mob, and, with their lives in their hands, defied it amid more terror than that of the battlefield. On the occasion of that sad event—the defeat that gave hope to rebels—the President, the cabinet, the veteran commander-in-chief, in a word, everybody, was filled with anxious concern, if not consternation. The press, the telegraph, the bulletin-boards of newspapers, every avenue of intelligence, was sought out by the inquiries of an excited people, filled with indignation, and flying to arms.

As Volta beheld the phenomenon of muscular contraction in the frog placed under electric influences, so now the nation's great heart throbbed, and by its powerful diastolic action, sent a mighty life-current throughout the whole body politic. Thousands of armed patriots rose at the call of their country, and were ready to march in regular array to the soul-inspiring notes of martial music, and were willing, in so holy a cause, to offer their lives a sacrifice on their country's altar, as in the days of the Revolution. The farmer left his fields, the artisan his handicraft, the doctor his patient, the lawyer his clients; the matron helped to buckle on her husband's knapsack, and the tender maiden hurried her betrothed to the seat of war, where, alas! many a young heart, beating high with hopes, ceased its pulses forever. It was thought the war would be of short duration. Four years did not see that gigantic rebellion subdued. But a great people had now determined, at any cost of life and treasure, to put it down, to crush it, to utterly exterminate the wicked from the land.

The author feels pride to be among the first, and he hopes to be among the last, of the patriot band that will give posterity a great, prosperous, undivided *Union*. May a grateful nation embalm the memories of her sons that bravely fought, and bled, and died, to perpetuate the Republic; may no widow of a brave soldier seek alms on the highway, or his children need to beg their bread; but honour, immortal honour be to patriots who rallied to their country's call, and went out as volunteers to drive back the foe! We may meet many of these one-armed and maimed heroes in our way through life, and let us never forget to cherish them with honour and esteem; some, past our kindness now, sleep in forgotten graves.

Oh, how many hearts, through the sad rebellion, have been totally crushed! But God is with the right; our cause is just, and we shall triumph. Many lives were sacrificed at an early period of the war, in the great battles of the Peninsula, and amid the pestilential swamps of Virginia, where McClellan so desperately struggled to maintain his own and his country's honour; that he was not superhuman, the nation at length realised; yet we think he gave the world evidence of possessing many of the attributes that go to make the great captain, though it was not his to command success. The leader of a mighty host, though one outnumbered, led his men with great valour, made a most masterly retreat from the York River to the James, and fully vindicated his fame in the great battles of Antietam and South Mountain.

Burnside, Hooker, and Meade, all in turn assumed command of the Army of the Potomac. The first, a distinguished soldier, was unsuccessful at Fredericksburg; the next, who, with his men, afterwards scaled Lookout Mountain and astonished the world, did not retire victorious from the bloody field of Chancellorsville. General Meade was now to command in that great fight that was to drive the defeated foe from the soil of Pennsylvania and Maryland. The soil had been desecrated by the tread of rebel soldiers, who ravaged the fields of these prosperous States, while the terrified inhabitants dreaded the approach of the ruthless invader. But a day of retribution was preparing.

Great changes had taken place in the army; the current of military events was varied. The Hon. Simon Cameron, Secretary of War, was succeeded by Hon. E. M. Stanton, who continues ably to discharge the responsible duties of his high station. The President had an able cabinet, and the efforts of the government were wisely directed, and accepted by the nation as an evidence that the rebellion would be crushed.

In obedience to the call of the President, the governors of the different States responded with promptitude with men to ward off invasion. New York sent out her troops. New Jersey her hardy sons, and the patriotic governor of Pennsylvania, Hon. A. G. Curtin, roused into action the militia for the defence of the State; while the fortifications on the Susquehanna formidably frowned on the invader, as significant of the warm reception lie would meet from bristling bayonets and polished guns, should he insult the honour of the State by an attack on its capital.

Thus, the sound of hostile invasion grew nearer and nearer, more and more distinct. The indications, that Pleasanton was the first to observe, of Lee's intention were now fairly developed—the enemy was on our soil in large force.

To meet him, the invincible legions that had seen service under McClellan and his successors in command—all able and valiant leaders—now were about to fight on their own soil, where valour and patriotism rose emulous of the bravery of Spartan heroism at Thermopylae, or the noblest struggle that history records.

We would wish to be able to do justice to the infantry that mainly composed the army at this great battle; but our present task is chiefly with the cavalry forces. All fought for the same end, animated by the same impulses.

The monuments that rose to departed heroes on this field, and the importance attached to success, evince the interest the nation felt in it; for a mischance here, might have blasted our hopes forever, and entailed on posterity this misery of an oligarchy usurping supreme power, and riveting the chain of the bondman. Among the patriots that distinguished themselves on the occasion, as they have on all occasions during the war, were the *surgeons*, whose skill and humanity ought never to be forgotten, for no class of men have served better or with purer motives.

The author *knows* this, being with them from the beginning of the struggle, and being conversant with all the good done, all the difficulties surmounted, all labours performed. The annals of surgery in no nation can point out higher triumph in the art; the hospitals have been founded on the best principles, and our nation has a right to feel proud of her medical men throughout the army. This testimony is forced from the author; for, though this volume is only intended as a detail of military affairs, too high a tribute cannot be paid to men, who, had they lived in other ages, like some of their profession, would have been honoured as deities.

The rebel General Stuart did not cross the Potomac with the main army of Lee; but, below Harper's Ferry, in the rear of our army, moved through Maryland a portion of his command, passing near the city of Washington, He safely eluded the columns sent out to intercept him, and, on the evening of the 29th of June, made his encampment five miles south of Hanover, Pennsylvania.

Thus far, his raid had been a success. But the following day he encountered obstacles he little expected. As before mentioned, that was the day on which General Kilpatrick had been put in command of a division of cavalry, with such men as Custer and Farnsworth to command his brigades, and Pennington and Elder his artillery.

The gallant General Farnsworth fell mortally wounded, a few days later, at the foot of Little Round Top, leading one of those daring cavalry charges which went so far towards saving the day at Gettysburg. The other three, Custer, Pennington, and Elder, made, by their deeds, during the next fifteen days, their names illustrious. While Stuart was ravaging the country for miles above his camp, Kilpatrick, with his young command, was rapidly marching towards the scene of desolation. Stuart had learned that the rebel General Ewell, who, for several days, had been at the town of York, had already hastily retreated towards Gettysburg to join Lee, who was marching for that point. This was unexpected to Stuart, and it necessitated a rapid movement on his part.

His object was, of course, to join the rebel army, and to do this without making a great detour, he must march through Hanover. The general was aware of all these facts, and, although greatly outnumbered, boldly formed his command in front of the town of Hanover, determined to dispute the advance of the rebel chief. The two forces met at 8 a. m., and a desperate battle ensued. For hours, it raged so fiercely that it was impossible to decide who would gain the day. Each in the fierce struggle put forth his mightiest efforts, and each seemed equally resolved to win or die.

In one of the many charges made throughout the day, Stuart led in person, broke through our lines, and had penetrated to the very centre of the town, when General Farnsworth, at the head of the Fifth New York, charged him in front and flank, and he was quickly driven from the streets. This was the only. time during the day that a single rebel soldier, save as a prisoner, polluted with his presence this loyal town.

At 4, p.m., the Fifth and Seventh Michigan came up fresh on the field, having taken no part in the fight, and were sent on the enemy's left. The leader waited till he saw the success of these two regiments, and then advanced his whole command. Stuart did not wait for the attack, but rapidly retreated towards York, his entire corps being thus whipped by a single division. The enemy's loss in this battle was very great; a battle-flag and a large number of prisoners were captured. Stuart moved rapidly by the town of York, and, by a long, circuitous route reached Lee's army near Gettysburg, escaping the pursuers that were after him, and were again destined to meet him. On the morning of the first of July, Buford passed through Gettysburg, met and engaged the rebel advance, a few miles beyond, and, by hard and skilful fighting, held him in check until a portion of our army, under Howard and Reynolds, came up. The gallant Reynolds fell in this day's battle, generally lamented.

An interesting scene presented itself as a portion of Buford's cavalry rode through the town. The young maidens of the place collected, dressed in white, and lined the principal streets on each side, waving flags and singing patriotic strains. Their sweet and melodious young voices rang forth a glad welcome, and the cavalry, as in passing the Pennsylvania line, found their spirits raised to the highest point of enthusiasm.

These peaceful scenes, however, were soon to be startled with the thunder of artillery, and the town and vicinity to become a Golgotha, where many a gallant heart, *"once pregnant with celestial fire,"* ceased its pulsations forever, and many a hitherto wakeful warrior *"slept that sleep that knows no waking,"* Tread gently on this sacred spot, and, as the place of burial tells to what State belong the patriots whose blood that day flowed freely for their country, and whose bones rest in peace where they fell, let the fire of patriotism rise in the heart with a higher flame, and, quenchless, continue to burn to all generations!

The author, as at Chancellorsville, was witness to the scenes of this great field on our own soil. For three days, the contest raged round the Pennsylvania College, whose medical department has sent out many thorough medical officers to the service, and whose department of arts furnished many youths who took arms in their hands, ere this eventful day, to meet the enemy; this college was a kind of centre, around which rolled the battle's wave and the work of death went on.

As when some frightful conflagration rages, and the devouring element, now here, now there, breaks forth from smouldering ruins, so the dire and terrific battle raged, till the last sounds of strife died away, and left behind the ghastly sight of a bloody battlefield, strewn with the wrecks of shattered humanity; and the profound silence that remained was only broken by the heart-rending cries of the wounded and dying. Even on the first day the hospitals were filled with the wounded, and it soon became evident at what a sacrifice of life the insolent foe would be chastised and fitly punished, routed, driven from our soil, and his shattered columns be forced from beyond the Potomac.

General Kilpatrick, who, at the quiet little town of Abbottsville, was resting his worn-out men and horses, after the hard fight with Stuart and the subsequent pursuit, heard, early on the morning of the 2nd of July, the thunder of artillery, which opened up the fight at Gettysburg on that day.

The echoes of that first discharge had scarce died away among the surrounding hills, when the clear notes of his bugles sent out the well-known and welcome sound, "To horse." Away dashed that splendid command, and, guided by the battle din, stopped not for any obstacle till it reached the scene of conflict. The sight presented defies all description; and, indeed, the clash of great armies contending for victory is attended with such circumstances of confusion, that baffles all attempts at regular order, in a series of events so thickly crowded together.

But mortal eye never beheld a spectacle more absorbing than that which now greeted the sight of this gallant cavalry commander, who rushed his well-tried battalions upon this field of blood, ready to take part, no matter how or at how much cost, in giving the enemy a Waterloo defeat.

The reputation of this general does not rest upon the deeds of this sanguinary conflict. Already the War Department knew his merits, and his friends, in the Senate and out of it, were aware of his prowess, his daring, and impetuosity that knew no restraint.

The author had that connection with the cavalry, at this period, that made him acquainted with the claims to distinction possessed by every leader. He intends no compliment to the young general, no eulogy, no attempt at an exaggeration—but would be impartial; and this feeling requires the admission, that on the bloody field of Gettysburg Kilpatrick made efforts, seconded by his brave command, whose memory should never fade so long as there are young American soldiers to be stimulated by glorious deeds of heroism.

In the absence of orders, his quick and almost intuitive perception pointed out the place where his presence was most needed. He did not wait for specific orders; he saw the enemy. Him to strike, so as to help the forces engaged, was the grand *desideratum*. He moved off, his right under General Farnsworth, to the right of our line, and engaged the enemy's cavalry at Hunterstown, the left of Lee's line of battle. Till late in the night, long after the two great armies had ceased to struggle, the roar of his artillery, the wild shout of his charging squadrons, and even the rattle of his small arms, as he continued successfully to battle with his old antagonists, Hampton, Lee, and Stuart, could be distinctly heard by the whole army, and told the Union general, as the noise of battle rolled in towards Gettysburg, that his right was safe.

Now ended, with this battle on the right, the second day's struggle. The veterans of the Army of the Potomac had contended with great valour for two days, led on by those able chiefs, who still hurled them on the foe, and in the terrible contest never thought of yielding an inch, but, if needs be, laying down their lives a sacrifice at the shrine of our glorious Republic.

With many brave men, a considerable number of gallant officers had fallen ere the sun of the second day, clouded with battle smoke, went down to rise the following day on a scene of carnage at the thought of which humanity recoils.

The sun rose bright and clear on the morning of the 3rd of July—a day long to be remembered by a grateful people. The weary army, that for two days had struggled so heroically against overwhelming numbers, arose on the morning of this day, fresh from the night's rest, and, like a lion, shook itself for the fray. All night long, when the soldier slept on his arms, dreaming of home and friends, the leaders were busily at work strengthening their lines, and making those important changes which, combined with the heroic bravery of our men, gave to us the victory. Buford was sent to Westminster, Gregg's Cavalry moved to the right of our line, and Kilpatrick, strengthened by the Regular Brigade, silently left this point, marched all night, and at daylight took up his position on our extreme left, beyond Little Round Top, with orders to charge the rebel infantry should an opportunity offer.

Everyone has read in the public prints the details of the battle which lasted three days, and we shall only allude to that portion of the battle of the third day in which the cavalry took a prominent part. On the extreme right, the cavalry, under Generals Gregg and Custer, had a most desperate engagement with the rebel General Stuart's entire corps, and gained in the end a most signal victory over him. Kilpatrick's cavalry had been skirmishing with the enemy since 10 a. m., and by 12 p. m. had forced its way far in upon the enemy's flank and rear, and was now ready to strike him.

An opportunity so to do soon offered. It was at 4 p. m. that a heavy force of rebel infantry moved out of the woods on the enemy's right, and rapidly passed toward the left of our main line of battle, with the evident intention of turning our position on Little Round Top.

The troops under Kilpatrick had drawn the sabre, and were about to charge this force in flank, when a second force equal in size to the first was seen rapidly approaching from the same direction, and a few minutes later a third line made its appearance. This was Longstreet's entire corps moving steadily forward to the charge. Having seen that if this charge was successful the day was lost, Kilpatrick resolved, no matter at what cost, to charge this formidable body of men in flank, and defeat, if possible, the rebel chiefs intention.

No time was to be lost; the Regular Brigade, under General Merritt, was pushed well in upon the left, while General Farnsworth, with the First Virginia, Eighteenth Pennsylvania and Fifth New York, was ordered to charge in flank the last of the rebel lines. This was General Hood's division, and had it not been for a low stone wall that intervened, this division would have been completely routed. As it was, our gallant cavalry rode over the wall, sabred the rebel infantry in the rear, and forced Hood to turn and face the wild rush of men and horse. Fresh regiments of cavalry were now sent in, when one line after another of Hood's splendid division gave way. Our cavalry halted not till a second wall and fresh line of infantry was reached. The rebel charging columns floated off towards the centre of our main line, and finally broke, and fled in confusion from under the terrible fire of artillery which now rained upon them from a hundred guns.

This was the last desperate effort of the rebel chief. Our tired and worn-out soldiers sank exhausted on the field so dearly won.

In this day's fight the cavalry won undying honours, but lost some of the truest, bravest men for which a nation ever mourned. These names are too numerous to mention; but we must pause to pay a tribute to the memory of one, whose career, so brilliant and glorious, tells us, in tearful words, that he died too soon for his country's good.

"Farnsworth"—so young, so generous, and so brave—of him Kilpatrick says, in his official report:

> In this charge fell the brave Farnsworth. Short and brilliant was his career. On the 29th of June a general, on the 1st of July he baptised his star in blood, and on the 3rd, for the honour of his young brigade and the glory of his corps, he yielded up his noble life.

We can say of him, in the language of another:

> Brave soldier, faithful friend, great heart—hail, and farewell!

Cavalry charge at Gettysburg, Pa., and death of General Farnsworth

CHAPTER 4

Kilpatrick Defeats the Rebels at Falling Waters

This important battle having ended in the victory of our arms, a general joy quickly diffused itself throughout the nation, as the telegraph announced the defeat of the rebel army and the news of their preparations to recross the Potomac, and place that river between them and our victorious forces.

The nation breathed free once more, and nothing now remained to be done, on the part of the victors, but follow up their success and cut off the rebel retreat, inflicting yet greater loss on, or capturing, their broken and retreating columns. Accordingly, a portion of Gregg's command was sent on the enemy's flank, in the direction of Chambersburg; while Kilpatrick, with his division and Colonel Hurey's brigade of Gregg's division, was directed to move in front of the rebel army, destroy wagon trains, burn bridges, and hold in check, in every way possible, the retreating rebel army.

At break of day, on the morning of the 4th of July, this officer put his column in motion, passed through Emmettsburg, and marched for the nearest point on the Gettysburg and Hagerstown road, intending to cross the mountain at Monterey. Rapidly he had marched all day long, and the head of his column had arrived within a few hundred yards of the Monterey House, on the top of the mountain, when the enemy, who had been made aware of this movement, had sent artillery and infantry to defeat it in this narrow mountain pass, opened with artillery and musketry, driving back the advance in confusion for several hundred yards.

General Kilpatrick now found himself in a very critical position, and, possibly, most men might have lost their presence of mind, or at least the calm and confident expression which, as a leader, has so much influence on the troops in the hour of danger.

Stuart attacked the rear, and the entire command, in one column, was upon a long, narrow, winding mountain road, with high, impassable bluffs upon the right, and deep, broad ravines upon the left. And to add to the difficulties of the position, it was raining in torrents, and no object could be distinguished in the midnight darkness.

We do not hesitate in saying, and have good reason to know, that had any want of firmness on the part of the leader, or any indecision or vacillation appeared, and a mischance occurred, this splendid command would then and there have been lost.

But with unflinching and steady purpose, bold bearing, and a mind equal to the emergency, the general rode to the head of the column, reassured his frightened people, and, notwithstanding the intense darkness that hid friend from foe, made such skilful dispositions and then attacked the hidden foe with such impetuosity that he fled in wild dismay, leaving his guns, a battle-flag, and four hundred prisoners in the victor's hands.

The pass was gained, and Pennington's and Elder's guns were soon echoing and re-echoing through the mountain defiles. The artillery opened thus on the flying columns of the routed foe, who, with wagons, ambulances, caissons, and the debris of a shattered army were rushing, in chaotic confusion, down the narrow mountain road, and scattering through the fields and woods on the plains below.

The general, by this daring movement, had now placed himself in advance of the rebel army, and all the following day was busily employed obstructing roads, pursuing and capturing detachment after detachment of the rebel troops scattered over the country, and burning wagon trains and other valuable property. In his official report, he says:

> On this day, I captured eighteen hundred and sixty prisoners, including many officers of rank, and destroyed the rebel General Ewell's immense wagon train, nine miles long.

At 4 p.m. the same day, he met and defeated the rebel General Stuart, in an engagement at Smithburg, which lasted one hour and forty minutes. Stuart that night retreated to Hagerstown, and Kilpatrick moved to Boonsboro', and encamped for the night.

After disposing of his prisoners and captured property to Major-General French, who was marching for, and whose advance had already reached. South Mountain Pass, Kilpatrick moved at daylight, on the morning of the 6th of July, to Hagerstown, surprised and defeated again the rebel General Stuart, who was forced to burn a large wagon train, to prevent its falling into our hands. Here the gallant Captain Dahlgren, of whom we shall afterwards make mention, lost, his leg, leading a most gallant charge.

Artillery firing was heard in the direction of Williamsport, and the messenger soon brought Kilpatrick word that this was General John Buford, who had crossed South Mountain Pass with his cavalry, and was now attempting to burn Lee's immense supply train, parked at Williamsport. Although the advance of the rebel infantry was known to be but a. few miles off, and rapidly moving, Kilpatrick quickly advanced at a trot, direct from Hagerstown, down the road to Williamsport, uniting his forces with Buford's.

Several hundred wagons were burned, and the whole train would have shared the same fate had it not been for the rebel infantry and cavalry, which now came up, and furiously attacked, in flank and rear, these two cavalry chiefs. Long and desperately did they contend with the overwhelming forces opposed to them—in fact, too long, for they were at one time completely enveloped, and nothing but their splendid generalship, and the indomitable bravery of their officers and men, saved them from capture and annihilation.

As it was, however, they successfully extricated themselves from their perilous position, recrossed the Antietam in safety, and encamped on the opposite side. We had several desperately wounded in this battle, and the author can never forget the anxiety in moving the hospital for retreat. On the morning of the 8th of July, the rebel cavalry, under Stuart, supported by infantry, advanced on Boonsboro', from Williamsport and Hagerstown, crossed the Antietam, drove our picket line, and at noon a furious battle was raging at Boonsboro'.

Buford had the right and Kilpatrick the left. The movements of the cavalry lines in this battle were among the finest sights the author remembers ever to have seen. It was here he first saw the young general, and little thought that one day the deeds he saw him perform he would transmit to paper and to posterity. Here, all day long, the rebel and the Union cavalry chiefs fought, mounted and dismounted, and striving in every manner possible to defeat and rout the other. The din and roar of battle that from 10 a.m. until long after dark had rolled over the plains and back through the mountains, told to the most anxious generals of them all, Meade and Lee, how desperate was the

47

struggle—Stuart and his men fighting for the safety of the rebel army, Buford and Kilpatrick for South Mountain's narrow pass.

Just as the setting sun sent his last rays over that dusty battlefield, Buford and Kilpatrick were seen rapidly approaching each other from opposite directions. They met; a few hasty words were exchanged, and away dashed Buford far off to the right, and Kilpatrick straight to the centre; and in less than twenty minutes, from right to centre, and from centre to left, the clear notes of the bugles rang out the welcome charge; and with one long, wild shout those glorious squadrons of Buford and Kilpatrick, from right to left, as far as the eye could see, in one unbroken line, charged upon the foe.

The shock was irresistible; the rebel line was broken—the routed enemy confessed the superiority of our men, as they fled from the well-fought field, leaving their dead and dying behind them; and our heroic chiefs led back their victorious squadrons, and, while resting on their laurels, gave their brave but wearied troops a momentary repose.

The following day, Meade's glorious army, the heroes of Antietam, South Mountain, and Gettysburg, debouched from South Mountain's rugged pass, moved out upon the plains below, and, on the evening of the 9th of July, encamped on the banks of the Antietam.

At 4 p.m., July 10th, Buford's Cavalry moved to Sharpsburg, the left of our line of battle, and Kilpatrick took a position on the extreme right, covering the road from Hagerstown to Gettysburg.

July 12th, this general, supported by Brigadier-General Ames' infantry, of Howard's corps, drove the enemy out of and occupied Hagerstown, thus contracting our lines many miles. For several days past, Lee had been making most desperate efforts to throw a bridge over the swollen waters of the Potomac, and escape to Virginia. In the meantime, however, he had taken up a strong natural position, and had spared no pains in adding to its strength by constructing lines of formidable earthworks.

On the 13th, General Meade finally decided to assault the rebel position. Orders to the various corps had been issued, the necessary dispositions completed, and the attack was to have been made on the 14th of July.

During the night of the 13th, General Kilpatrick, while examining his picket line, became convinced, from certain well-known indica-tions, that the enemy was leaving his front. He at once dispatched a courier to the headquarters of his chief with this information, and then, without waiting for orders, assembled his command at 3 o'clock

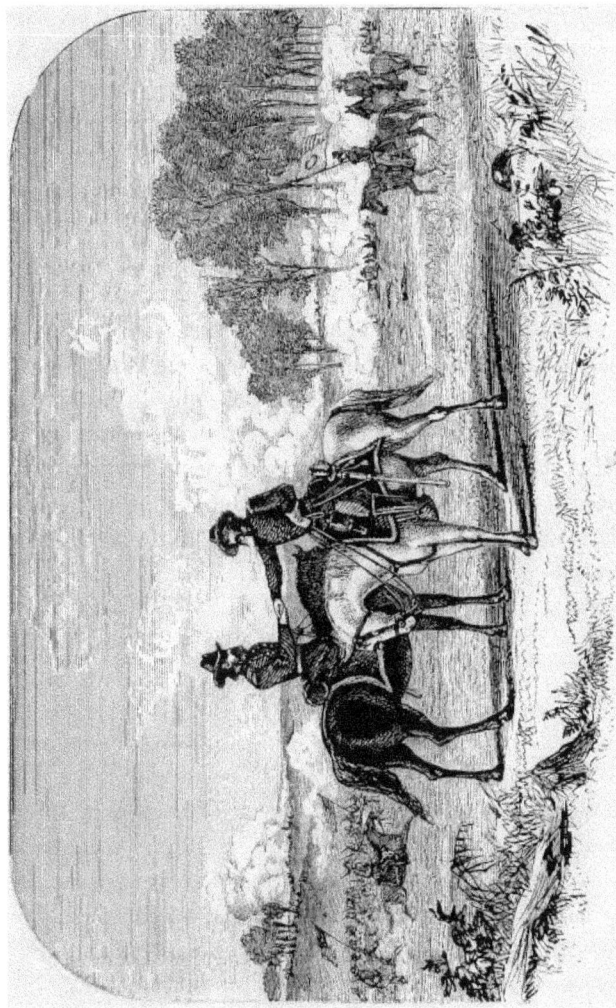

Generals Kilpatrick and Buford at the Battle of Boonsboro'

a. m., was in motion, and at 7 a.m. charged and drove a portion of the rear guard of the enemy into the Potomac at Williamsport. He then pushed rapidly down the river, and came upon the enemy's rear guard, one mile from Falling Waters, consisting of a division of infantry, under the command of Major-General Pettigrew.

So quickly had Kilpatrick come upon this general, that he was taken totally by surprise, his artillery captured before it could be placed in position, and Pettigrew himself killed in a sabre charge made by Major Weber, of the Sixth Michigan.

For a long time did this veteran division of infantry struggle to beat back the gallant cavalry, but finally broke and fled, in wild disorder, unable longer to resist the rapid and persistent charges of our men, and the destructive fire from Pennington's artillery.

In this battle, upwards of fifteen hundred prisoners, two guns, and three battle-flags were captured, and the ground was covered with killed and wounded rebels. Thus, ended this fight at Falling Waters.

The enemy had been driven from the free soil of the North; and we challenge the world to produce a career more brilliant than that of the young cavalry general, whose deeds we have recounted from the moment he gave the insolent rebel his first check at Hanover Farm, through the fifteen splendid victories which followed in the space of so many days, up to the moment, when, at Falling Waters, he struck him a last terrible and parting blow.

In his official report, he says:

In this campaign, my command has captured forty-five hundred prisoners, nine guns, and eleven battle-flags!

The splendid career of our cavalry under Custer, Merritt, and Torbett, in the Shenandoah Valley, may equal, but does not surpass, the brilliant record of Kilpatrick's Third Cavalry Division in this campaign. The author, as well as the candid reader, cannot solve the mystery that another star was not added to the one this general so well earned; but if our conquering young hero had but one star, we shall show, in the following chapters, that it was in the ascendant, rose high in the firmament, the wonder and admiration of the nation.

The enemy was now chased from the free soil which he had so insolently entered a few weeks before. The audacity of the rebels was confounded, their forces routed, their hopes blasted. Had the expedition of Lee proved successful, had the skill of our commanders and bravery of our soldiers been unequal to the task, hopes might have been given to the false confederacy, and its chief been interfering with the laws that govern free men, or been dictating terms in the national capital.

Fancy may paint to the thoughtful what must have ensued, had a rebel general, flushed with victory, captured the cities of Baltimore and Washington, New York and Philadelphia, and issued his edicts to the nation from its own capital. Yet such an event might have happened had Lee's invasion proved a success; for, that he had friends and partisans in both Maryland and Pennsylvania, who will be bold enough to deny? The truth is, had he not been beaten at Gettysburg, the event, in all probability, might have been fatal to freedom. The events herewith connected are of great interest to the future historian, and, in time, the battle of Gettysburg, with all the secret history of the rebellion, will have been written out. And an interesting history it will make.

The importance of the cavalry will then be more fully seen than now, and reasons strong and satisfactory appear why, at this present period, many facts were kept unrevealed from the public. The enemy was now in rapid retreat through Virginia, pursuing his way through the valley towards Staunton and Gordonsville. His loss was immense, and he departed from free soil greatly weakened and severely punished, and only too glad to escape in a manner very different from the audacious way in which he first crossed the Potomac. The people became more united than ever before, and new recruits were everywhere received into the Union ranks, and continued to swell the numbers devoted to the strength of the government and the salvation of the Union. Many men thought the rebellion would collapse; but the authorities at Washington persevered in their efforts to crush it out, and Congress adopted the measures calculated to attain the desired end

CHAPTER 5

West Point

General Meads in a short time followed up Lee's army, as it was not the intention of the leaders, who had driven the rebels across the Potomac, to allow them any time for rest, but to keep them constantly on the move, and watch them with a vigilant eye. There is, however, a limit to the endurance which men and horses are capable of, and, beyond this, the overtaxed powers give way, and exhausted nature claims her rights. The great mental and physical exertions of General Kilpatrick, continued through a series of battles, and rapid movements, marches, and evolutions, might astonish any one capable of judging the severity required in the performance of duties with rigid military exactness, continued night and day.

It will not, be surprising that even his iron frame was not proof against the fatigues of camp, prolonged through the hardships and sufferings of a soldier's life for a protracted period in the events before recorded. Few there are, except those who have had experience, who know how much privation the brave soldier and his general suffer in the toils of the field, on the rapid march, the hasty bivouac, the broken slumbers, the wakeful watching, and the scanty fare—all submitted to without a murmur by the veteran who sleeps on his arms in the face of the enemy, and endured with magnanimity by his general, who often never closes his eyes in "*Tired nature's sweet restorer—balmy sleep.*"

The exhausted energies of General Kilpatrick required a season of rest, which a troublesome inflammatory complaint and general debility rendered imperative. Has division, therefore, was placed under the temporary command of General Custer, and parting with his command for a season, he bent his way to New York and the Highlands of the Hudson, and at West Point spent some weeks of rest, enjoying the tender assiduities of his friends. The division, meantime, under Custer, marched with the main army of the Potomac in pursuit of Lee, and then encamped at the romantic and pleasant town of Warrenton.

While General Kilpatrick was enjoying the rest and invigorating breezes on the banks of the Hudson, and receiving the congratulations of his admirers, the command was receiving those supplies necessary to an army; clothing, equipments, arms, and subsistence for the next campaign, were being furnished in abundance.

The cavalry rested and recruited its strength, till, duly prepared. General Pleasanton made his splendid dash into Culpepper. This will be duly described in a future page; but we will at present take a look up the Hudson, where the general is on leave. While he is resting at West Point, among scenes so beautiful, almost without a parallel, we may linger with him awhile, to see how, having hung up his sword in the peace of the domestic home, where the agreeable society of his beautiful and accomplished wife and prattle of his noble boy—the pledge of love and affection—soon restored his spirits, improved his health, and filled his being with higher aspirations.

You, husbands and fathers, who have parted with your loved ones, and gone forth to do battle for the Union on the dangerous fields of strife, who have visited in dreams the scenes dearest to you on earth, and, in fancy, pressed the loved ones to your heart, but whom the midnight sound of the bugle routes from the hasty bivouac to drive back the foe—you can tell what joy fills the soul when a leave of absence releases you for a time, and, not in vision, but reality, you strain the loved ones to your breast in a long and fond embrace.

The mighty waters of the Hudson, rolling in silent grandeur past the great City of New York, visited no happier household than that of the young general whom we have followed from the tented field to the peaceful shades of home. We are pleased to see him happy, and shall not approach too near, but, leaving him to his paradise with his Eve, content ourselves with marking the place where so many associations of interest abound. Come with us, reader, to this spot of the nation's care, where so many gallant spirits, like Kilpatrick, learned those great military principles which have since made them famous.

That we may have, at one sweep of the eye, a scene beautiful, grand, magnificent beyond description, let us climb Fort Putnam's rugged side, and stand upon her crumbling battlements that for years have slowly yielded stone and mortar to driving storms and winter frosts, till now but little is left of that old structure, save rugged lines of fast crumbling walls, and huge, shapeless masses of earth and stone. Dear to

RESIDENCY OF GENERAL KILPATRICK, AT WEST POINT, ON THE HUDSON

us is this old fort—proud relic of the glorious past! As we stand here, on this airy mount, and gaze down upon the scene below, what grand old memories of the past come rushing back upon the mind! Here once centred the nation's hopes; here an Arnold hatched his treason; and here the great Washington breathed forth his patriotic prayers. Where the white tents of the cadets' encampment now are seen, once stood the rude huts of the soldiers of the Revolution.

And the splendid and formidable forts only serve to show the stranger where those old redoubts and earthworks stood, that once made West Point the bulwark of the Hudson.

What an appropriate spot for the nation's military school, as the young cadet paces his lonely rounds, or wanders amid towering monuments, fitly erected here in honour of the heroes of the past!

What high hopes and resolves must fill his breast, and what aspirations must be his to follow in their footsteps and emulate their renown. In this place, a few years ago, young Kilpatrick came as an humble "*plebe*," passed through the severe ordeal of military training, and finally graduated honourably to himself and Mends.

But two years have passed, and he returns to his *alma mater* again, a *general*, to receive the congratulations of his friends; and, what was more, the approbation of his instructors and professors, who, next to him, were proudest of his honours.

West Point delights to honour those of her sons who are true to her and a credit to the nation. How so many of her children, nursed on her lap, imbibing nutrition from her precepts and nestled in her bosom, could take the wrong path, prove recreant to her teachings, and arm against the old flag, it is difficult to her loyal sons to comprehend, and is to be accounted for only by those fatal heresies and delusions of Southern supremacy and superiority, with which the minds of the youth of the South were so thoroughly imbued from their earliest susceptibilities of instruction.

The honourable reception accorded to General Kilpatrick, on his return to West Point, proves the kind interest taken by all in his fame, success, and welfare. The respect and congratulations of the professors were an honour to anyone. We have only to allude to Professor Bartlett, the man of science, whose books on Mechanics and Philosophy have earned him a wide reputation; Professor Mahan, the great engineer and genuine American, who, at the Court of St. James, so nobly sustained our national character; Professor Church, the distinguished teacher of Mathematics, whose Calculus and Analytical Geometry are so highly valued as text-books; Professor Weir, whose artistic skill the author, like everybody, had occasion to admire in the paintings in the national capitol; the kind and warm-hearted chemist.

Professor Kendricks; Professor Angell, the gentlemanly and accomplished French scholar and instructor—so kind, and truly esteemed by the cadets; Professor French, Ethical Instructor and Chaplain of the Post, who united the young graduate in holy matrimony with her he loved, and a few months later performed the melancholy office of reading the burial service over her grave. These, and many more, received their student back again with open arms, and rejoiced over his success.

Thus, the Higher Mathematics, Mechanics, and Philosophy, Chemistry, Mineralogy, Geology, Civil and Military Engineering, Military Science, French, Spanish, International Law, Belles-Lettres, Logic, Mental and Moral Science—subjects so well taught here with great ability, in a spot which Plato might have chosen for the Academus— all these subjects, and many more in which he was well versed, again brought to mind and convinced the subject of this volume how much advantage, in common with others, he had reaped at this celebrated National Academy.

From intimate relations with General Kilpatrick, we are well acquainted with his devotion to his *alma mater*, and of the great respect he entertains for this celebrated institution, which has sent out no truer son, nor one more fitted to reflect the honours that its reputation and scholarship entitle him to. And not on the battlefield only has he done credit to her teachings. On one of his visits near Rutger's College, N. J., that institution conferred on him the degrees of Bachelor and Master of Arts in a manner highly flattering and duly appreciated. He was about once more to buckle on his sword and return to the field. His health was restored, and his active spirit led him again towards it, in the path of duty.

His companion, so fondly cherished, he was destined to see no more; he might become honoured and renowned, wear laurels of victory and be praised for success, but they would not be shared with her much longer; and, vain renown! the fondest hopes of his heart and pride of his life were destined, like the lovely flower nipped by the frost, or broken from the parent stem, to decay, to die!

The general, on his return to his command, still at Warrenton, was received with joy and enthusiasm by his brave troops; and, responsive to the clarion-note of war again sounding, he was prepared once more to lead his gallant squadrons to the field.

The following passage from the valedictory address to which allusion has been made, will show his principle of action, and clearly point out his selection of the true course which alone leads to greatness:

Friends of the corps, you of the second class, and who are soon to graduate, and you who have years yet before you: let me say, for your encouragement, that I have often thought, as one difficulty after another has been met, and year after year has passed slowly by, if I would ever receive a reward for all my labours.

But now I answer, Yes! the intelligent and smiling faces of my comrades answer. Yes! Persevere, then, gentlemen. Your time will come, and so will your reward. The future is before you as well as me. All of us think of it, and attempt to trace from time to time the course we would follow; yet how few of us will ever realise the bright anticipations of worldly honours or military glory.

And, suppose we should? What then? What would it all amount to? What is all the false glory worth that clusters for a time about the corrupt political hero's brow? Who would give aught for the empty shout of a populace, and who envies the tottering position gained through false ambition and a people corrupt?

These sentiments were such as in the commencement of his career animated the young orator. They formed a basis of action, and seeing the path of true glory, sought it in the service of his country, 'neath the old flag, while some who heard him missed the way, and pierced their breasts with many sorrows.

CHAPTER 6

Desperate Battle and Victory at Culpepper, etc.

The rebel General Lee now had his headquarters at Orange Court-House, and the main body of his army was encamped on the south side of the Rapidan. Stuart, however, was encamped about Culpepper, picketing the Rappahannock. A general advance of our army was decided upon about the middle of September. General Pleasanton was directed to cross the Rappahannock, and engage the rebel cavalry. Accordingly, he broke camp at an early hour, and crossed the Rappahannock at three points: Gregg at Sulphur Springs, Buford at Rappahannock Bridge, and Kilpatrick at Kelley's Ford.

On the plains of Brandy Station these various columns united.

Kilpatrick arrived first and had a sharp skirmish with the enemy. Pleasanton, with Buford's and Gregg's divisions, pushed straight on Culpepper, driving the enemy before him, while Kilpatrick was directed to move off across the country, and attack Culpepper in the direction of Stevensburg.

Stubbornly the enemy fought, and finally, within less than a mile of the town, succeeded in checking the advance of Buford and Gregg. For a long time, at this point, the enemy baffled every attempt to dislodge him from his strong position; but finally, when all began to wonder what had become of Kilpatrick, his flags appeared on the hills far to the left of Culpepper, and directly his artillery opened on the enemy's rear, who at once fell back into the town.

Giving them no time to form, or make new dispositions, he charged them with the First Vermont, Harris Light Cavalry, Fifth New York, and First Michigan. The town was carried, in spite of a heavy fire from the artillery; three Blakely guns were captured, and the enemy chased in total rout from the streets, General Custer leading in person the First Vermont.

A few moments later, and Buford's and Gregg's divisions also came into the town. Buford passed rapidly out on the road towards Poney Mountain, and Gregg pursued the enemy to Rapidan Bridge. The following day Pleasanton occupied the various fords on the Rapidan.

Again, had our cavalry beaten the Southern chivalry, on the same broad plains that witnessed their defeat a few months before. The Army of the Potomac now advanced, crossed the Rappahannock, the Union general making his head-quarters at Culpepper, while the cavalry guarded the flanks and rear.

Gregg took up his position at Rappahannock Bridge, Buford at Stevensburg, and Kilpatrick the right, with his headquarters at James City. In October, Lee, who had been encamped at Orange Court-House, crossed the Rapidan, moved to Madison Court-House, and, by a flank movement to our right, forced Meade to retire, first to the Rappahannock, and afterwards to Centreville, the enemy covering the rear.

We are pleased now to recount one of the most splendid achievements of the war. As the army fell back from Culpepper, Major-General Pleasanton, who had previously given his orders, remained at that point to watch and direct the movements of his cavalry. Gregg, who had been brought up and sent forward towards Cedar Mountain, to assist in the retrograde movement, fell back to Culpepper, passing out on the road towards Sulphur Springs. An hour later, and Kilpatrick reached Culpepper, and slowly retired towards his old and glorious field, Brandy Station, marching on a line with Buford, who was now falling back from Racoon Ford, and had at this time reached Stevensburg, being heavily pressed by the rebel cavalry under Fitzhugh Lee. Kilpatrick had scarce moved a mile from Culpepper, when his rear was furiously attacked by Hampton's division of cavalry, commanded by General Stuart in person.

General Pleasanton was with Kilpatrick's command on this occasion; General Davis's brigade had the right, and General Custer's the left. Slowly, but safely, this command fell back, under the direction of these celebrated cavalry generals. Buford had been forced to fall more rapidly back, before the overwhelming forces of Lee, than had Kilpatrick; so that when the latter reached his old battlefield of Brandy Station, he found that Buford had already passed beyond towards the Rappahannock. His right was entirely exposed. In fact, long lines of rebel cavalry were already forming in his front, and Fitzhugh Lee's batteries, from the hills on the right, soon opened on his flank with terrible effect, Buford, unaware of Kilpatrick's position, had fallen back, and the rebel General Fitzhugh Lee's division of cavalry held, in three lines, the only road over which our troops could pass.

To add to the peril of the situation, Stuart had rapidly passed from the rear to Kilpatrick's left, and was fast enveloping his entire command. Our troops, now alarmed at the formidable dispositions being rapidly made to secure their capture, cast their anxious eyes on their lion-hearted leader, and when they saw how coolly he gave his orders, how boldly he rode on the elevated ground, in full view of friends and foes, his battle-flag proudly floating by his side, they no longer doubted the issue of the contest; their brave hearts, that for a moment ceased to beat, again sent the life-blood coursing through their veins, and with pale, compressed lips and flashing eyes waited for the order that brought three thousand blades leaping from their scabbards; and, as the glittering brands danced out upon the sunlight, one long, wild shout of proud defiance rolled out from that body of brave men, telling the host of rebel horsemen that their task had scarce begun.

In three heavy columns, of a thousand each, the intrepid leader formed his men, and slowly moved down upon the foe, while the heavy line of skirmishers on front, flanks, and rear, held back the eager enemy, and while from out the intervals the batteries of Pennington and Elder opened huge gaps in those strong rebel lines. General Custer and his staff rode upon the left, General Davis on the right, while Generals Pleasanton and Kilpatrick rode in the centre.

When within a few hundred yards of the rebel lines, our band struck up our great national air, "*Yankee Doodle*," and a hundred bugles rang forth the charge. The boasted chivalry of the South, who there had gathered confident of victory, had not the moral courage to witness long this vast array of flashing sabres, but broke in wild dismay, and opened wide a road, over which passed our gallant squadrons, uniting with the men of Buford on the hill beyond.

The rebel cavalry, ashamed of their own cowardly conduct, reorganised, and now commenced that last great cavalry battle on the plains of Brandy Station, which was to decide, and forever, the question of superiority.

No one, save those who witnessed that fight, can begin to imagine the deeds of daring done. Pleasanton, Buford, Kilpatrick, Custer, and Davis, again and again in person led the charges; until long after night

Major-General Pleasonton and his generals meeting on the hill beyond Culpepper, after the victory over Stuart

the contest lasted, when the foe, tired and exhausted by his fruitless efforts, ceased his attacks, and our cavalry, unmolested, gathered up their dead and wounded, and in safety crossed the Rappahannock.

Now the army fell back to Centreville, Buford moving with the train, Gregg in the rear of the centre, and Kilpatrick on the left of Major-General Warren's Corps, while the enemy moved to Bristow Station and commenced the destruction of the railroad. After waiting several days for the enemy to attack, General Meade finally concluded to advance.

Accordingly, he put his army in motion, and found that the enemy had crossed the Rappahannock. The rebel cavalry, however, under Stuart, had remained near Buckland Mills, and here Kilpatrick, who had the advance of our army, had a severe engagement with a whole rebel corps, and here he met his first and only reverse, and only saved his command by the great personal efforts he made that day. He succeeded, however, in reaching our lines in safety and without the loss of a single gun, with his organisations preserved. His command that day did not number two thousand effective fighting men, while the enemy had upon the field two large divisions and sixteen guns.

Our army now moved to the Rappahannock, while the enemy encamped on the opposite bank.

On the first day of November our army crossed the river, and the enemy fell back through Stevensburg, and Culpepper, to and across the Rapidan, and went into position on the opposite side. Buford moved to Culpepper, Kilpatrick to Stevensburg, and the army went into winter-quarters near Brandy Station.

Here the cavalry remained until the grand movements in the spring, under Lieutenant-General Grant, and nothing occurred worthy of interest save the noble effort made by General Kilpatrick to rescue our prisoners on Belle Isle and the various prisons of Richmond. This we will proceed to describe after we speak of that sad event in his life which at this time took place, and cast a sombre shade over the success of that victorious and popular general. The melancholy event to which we allude is the loss of her whose name is inscribed on his banner and in his heart His beloved wife, Alice, the guiding star of his life, for whom, perhaps more than for himself, animated and cheered by her inspiring spirit, he sought glory and military renown.

Pass we over the sorrows of his heart whom she left to mourn, and the tearful sadness of those her attached friends, and the bereaved hearts that followed and committed her lovely clay to the last resting-place, where, in a few short weeks, the darling boy, too, slept by his mother's side! Her memory is embalmed in the hearts that loved her, and recollections, like the fragrance of flowers strewn on the place of her rest, draw forth the tributary tear. Lines written by Miss Jennie Gray, upon the death of her friend, Mrs. General Kilpatrick.

The chief wins laurels for his brow,
His name is heard on every tongue;
His deeds of glory, written now,
Shall by immortal bards be sung.

What shall that proud, high spirit tame,
E'en to forget his native land?
He battles not for wealth or fame;
What, then, shall palsy that young hand?

In yonder rooky dell there pines
The cherished idol of his soul;
She weeps and prays beneath the pines,
Nor can her cherished boy console.

Sweet pitying angels o'er bend;
Send me to guard my love, she cries,
When gently life's fair veil they rend,
And to her Lord the Seraph flies.

He saw her not! the lightning stroke,
That paralyzes heart and brain.
Upon that Warrior's head has broke.
Oh! what can thrill and fire again?

Alas! what were the laurels that decked and were yet more profusely to adorn the young general's brow? Wife, child, all were gone; but here, with a brighter lustre, shone out the inherent love of country and humanity so deeply implanted in a wounded crushed heart! For the noble spirit of General Kilpatrick made a mighty effort worthy of true greatness.

Here was the sublime spectacle of a triumph of the mind—of the soul over circumstance—giving the power, with the help of the Almighty, to overcome private griefs, rise above personal sorrow, and to conceive the noblest idea of a lofty and humane purpose. He compassed the intention, and endeavoured to execute the grand design of liberating our prisoners, whose known sufferings were the people's grief, and restoring them again to friends, home, and liberty.

CHAPTER 7

Rebel Inhumanity and Cruelty

The restraint of personal freedom is hard to be borne, and nothing, perhaps, weighs heavier on the human heart than deprivation of liberty and incarceration in a prison-cell. The prison at Rome did more to break the fierce spirit of Jugurtha, probably, than all the perils he ever encountered. The very name of the *Bastille* is calculated to chill the heart of the feeling, and fill the mind with a shuddering but indefinite apprehension.

The author has felt a deep interest in visiting that ancient fortress, built by the Norman conqueror to awe his subjects, and could not see, without emotion, the little prison-cell that confined the great Raleigh for years. Instruments of torture are yet to be seen in this tower, and though not now used, they tell a tale of the past.

When the "benevolent Howard" visited the prisons of Europe, he found thousands of human creatures living in a condition of fearful degradation, hopelessness, and utter wretchedness—who dragged out a miserable existence till relieved by kind death, that freed them from the yoke of bondage.

Our prisons now are upon a scale of humanity and liberality, and confinement from the air and sun, the green fields, and pleasant objects that delight the eye, are among the worst things a prisoner usually has to dread.

One would think the day had gone by in which prisoners would meet with ill treatment scarcely less cruel than the instruments of torture in past ages. Civilization, in this latter half of the nineteenth century, might enable us to indulge the hope that cruelty to prisoners would be a thing unheard of; but, if all the history about our brave men and officers captured by the enemy were fully disclosed, it would draw tears from every eye and a compassionate sigh from the hardest heart. How many would be found to have languished and idled, for mere want of food, in the filthy precincts of the Libby Prison, the execrable atmosphere of Castle Thunder, or the yet more fearful confines of Belle Isle! Many a shadow, like the ghost of Hamlet's father, might truly say of the secrets of his prison-house:

I could a tale unfold, whose lightest word
Would harrow up thy soul, freeze thy young blood.
Make thy two eyes, like stars, start from their spheres,
Thy knotted and combined locks to part,
And each particular hair to stand on end,
Like quills upon the fretful porcupine!

This is no exaggeration; confinement, filth, and *starvation* sent many to their long homes; and, if liberated, they returned, mere skeletons, to their friends and loved ones, in time only to die.

The rebels, in many cases, stripped the prisoners of almost all their clothing, and often left them entirely destitute. Hardy and powerful was that frame that could bear the trying ordeal, of which, though not so long confined there as others, the author can speak feelingly, having also been a captive in the filthy Libby Prison.

It seems that the longer the war lasted the worse treatment did the prisoners receive. The poor creatures seemed to experience no pity or compassion from their cruel and hard-hearted jailors, and many died actually for want of food We do not mean to say that in every case the treatment was bad. We experienced courtesy, and received proper supplies at Staunton and at Lynchburg, and acknowledged the same in the public papers at the time of release. For a long time, we contended that the accounts of bad treatment of Federal prisoners was perhaps exaggerated; but the truth became, alas I only too evident, and with shame we are compelled to record it, that the manner in which the rebels treated the poor prisoners in their power, is a disgrace to humanity and a blot and stigma on the false Confederacy forever that cannot be effaced.

At this period, numerous prisoners who had fought for the preservation of the Union on the glorious battlefields the memory of which will render their names immortal in the annals of their country, were now captives among the cruel foe, and spent their wearisome days and nights in pining and languishing confinement, set off from their brave and victorious companions, and with but feeble hopes of ever seeing their homes again, or once more basking in the sunlight of liberty.

No! they felt that these blessings were not for them, and the horrors of their imprisonment intensified those saddening thoughts.

Prompted by feelings of humanity and compassion for fellow-soldiers thus suffering under the brutality practised upon them by a cowardly and cruel foe, capable of inflicting the most atrocious and inhuman barbarities upon men, whose valour as soldiers, only too well known to their captors, as well as the treatment always accorded by a civilized enemy to his prisoners, entitled them to proper care and protection, General Kilpatrick determined to effect their release.

The difficulties in the way, however, were so great as to seem almost insurmountable, and the gallant leader well knew the perils to himself and men that strewed every foot of ground with ambush, captivity, and death, and might, in the failure of the enterprise, consign them all to the tender mercies of the enemy, more fearful than the liveliest fancy can portray. The men were willing to follow their leader, despite dangers, toil, or death, reliant on his prowess and skill, prepared to gain the glorious end or nobly perish in the attempt.

Self-reliant, and fired with noble feelings, he animated his proud cavalrymen with his own spirit, which he breathed into them till the fire of patriotism, glowing on the altar of their hearts, shot out with enthusiastic blaze, and, when the kindled flame had risen to the desired point, waved his well-tried sabre at the head of this brave band of picked men, and off they started in the perilous but determined path of death or glory. Some have made the assertion, and not without due foundation, that General Kilpatrick is *ambitious.*

Such he is for name, for fame, and for the success of the cause in which he draws his sword. We could wish that more of our generals were like him in this respect; for, is it not possible, that some may think far too much of ease and comfort, and too little of glory? But, if he has any enemies, and few men are without some, the most bitter of them cannot say that, on this occasion, he was actuated by any other motive than that of performing a great and good act—an act that would bring down fervent, heart-felt blessings on his head from his suffering comrades in prison and their anxious friends at home.

Never did Christian knight of old ride forth to battle with the fierce *infidel*, on the plains of Palestine, with purer, holier purpose, unmixed with self or self-interest, than did he who risked life, liberty, and fame, to give freedom to others.

It is not our purpose to state in this work, how, or why, or through whose neglect, this great expedition did not succeed. The time has not yet come for the secret history of this war to be made public; but the want of success attending this noble enterprise is not to be attributed to any fault, or want of skilful and daring efforts, on the part of its leader. We could, perhaps, point out where the difficulty lies, being in possession of data; but our object is to give a plain narrative of the events attending this grand design, whose want of success, to all impartial readers, will not lessen the moral heroism the humblest private in those ranks may be said to have possessed. The idea originated with General Kilpatrick, and, on being submitted, in all its plans and details, met the approbation of the Honourable Secretary of War and of the President of the United States.

It was indeed a hazardous enterprise; but the great object to be attained justified the attempt, and everyone knew and admitted that if anyone could succeed, it was he who now risked the reputation he had before, on many a dangerous field, so dearly won.

On the twenty-eighth day of February, 1864, just as tattoo was sounding through the camps that dotted the plain and hill side, and the Army of the Potomac was about to sink to rest, the daring leader of this undertaking, with four thousand men of tried bravery, bade *adieu* to kind friends and comrades of the army, silently left their camp about Stevensburg, and marched for Ely's Ford, on the Rapidan.

Rebel pickets watched this ford, and lined the opposite side. Colonels Dahlgren and Cook had the advance, with five hundred chosen men. When within a few hundred yards of the ford, the column halted. A few low, hasty orders were given, and then, silently, fifty resolute men were seen to separate and move off in the direction of the river. For upwards of an hour the column halted, and officers and men, in low whispers, asked each other: "why don't we move; what can be the matter?"

Soon a number of dark objects were seen approaching from the direction of the ford. A horseman rode out from the column, and the low, firm challenge, "Halt! Who comes there?" brought back the quick, sharp reply: "Hogan, General; the rebel picket is all right."

This explained the delay. The daring and skilful scout, Hogan, had crossed his men at different points above and below the ford, one at a time, and silently surrounded and captured, without firing a gun, the rebel captain, lieutenant, and twenty-two men, stationed there to guard the ford and give alarm. It may interest the reader to know that the same scout—whose romantic and daring history would fill a volume—took prisoners, during this raid, at Frederick Hall, consist-

MEETING OF GENERAL KILPATRICK AND THE SCOUT HOGAN, AT MIDNIGHT AT ELY'S FORD

ing of a rebel colonel, two majors four captains, seven lieutenants, and four or five men. This was done by a complete surprise, with twenty men only, the enemy having sixty pieces of artillery and a regiment of infantry within three hundred yards. The scout is at this moment escaped from prison, having seen some of the most astonishing adventures.

The column now rapidly but silently crossed the river, marched all night, and at daylight was passing through Spottsylvania Court-House, and was now twenty miles in the rear of the entire rebel army, having passed in safety through its lines, with that large body of horsemen; ambulances, and artillery; and not a shot had been fired to alarm the vigilant sentinel or tell the rebel chief that four thousand Yankee horsemen, with artillery, were marching through his camp, who, ere the setting of another sun, would be thundering at the gates of his capital city.

The most difficult feat was now accomplished. Repressing the exultant shout that his men seemed determined to give when they learned their great success, the leader dashed on towards Beaver Dam Station, on the Virginia Central Railroad. At twelve o'clock heavy reports were heard in the direction of Frederick Hall Station, informing the general that Dahlgren had struck the railroad near that point, and was using torpedoes in the destruction of the road.

Colonels Dahlgren and Cook had been in advance with five hundred men, to destroy the railroad and telegraph near Frederick Hall, and, if prudent, attempt to capture a large park of artillery encamped at that point; moved to Goochland Court-House, crossed the James River, thence down the south bank, destroying the Bologne arsenal, across James River, leading into Richmond, and just below Belle Isle, at nine o'clock the following morning. This accomplished, the prisoners on Belle Isle could easily join Dahlgren in the city, and assist in forming a junction with the general, who intended to enter the city at the same time by the Brook Pike. Kilpatrick reached and destroyed Beaver Datam Station, four p.m., and went into camp for a few hours at eight p.m., nine miles from Ground Squirrel Bridge, on the South Anna, and on the road to Richmond.

Learning that a heavy force of the enemy were guarding the railroad bridge over the South Anna, as well as the road bridge, a few miles above, four hundred and fifty men, under Major Hall, were sent to make a feigned attack on this force, diverting the attention of the enemy from the main columns, which safely crossed the South Anna, at daylight had crossed the Fredericksburg Railroad, and reached the Brook Pike, and at 9 a. m. had boldly attacked and carried the enemy's first line of works, and from a point less than two miles from the city the artillery had opened on the enemy's works.

This was the signal agued upon; but no answering signal came. The general had resolutely and skilfully carried out the plans matured long before he left his camp at Stevensburg, and, as he promised, had reached, and fired a shot, on the hour agreed upon, at the city of Richmond.

And as the echoes of that shot reached the ears of the great arch-traitor, first informing him and his trembling guards that an enemy was thundering at the gates of his city, it also reached the ears of seventeen thousand brave soldiers, who, for long months, had endured every suffering in Libby Prison, Castle Thunder, and at Belle Isle.

Shout after shout sent back the echo, and prayer after prayer went up from the hearts of those anxious, grateful men, that the efforts made for their deliverance might be crowned with success.

Several hours were now passed in reconnoitring the works, which were found to be formidable and well manned; and it having been finally learned that the enemy's infantry from Bottom's Bridge, which it was expected would be detained at that place, had actually been brought to the city, and were now marching into position to dispute his advances, and hearing nothing from Dahlgren, General Kilpatrick, at dark, withdrew, crossed the Chickahominy at the Meadow bridge, and went into camp.

A heavy storm of sleet and hail, and, at times, snow, now set in, drenching to the skin the tired and worn-out soldiers. But, despite the fatiguing march and the want of co-operation, the unsuccessful attempt to enter the city, and the cold, driving storm, the general determined to make one more attempt to carry off our prisoners.

His scouts had come in, reporting that they had actually been within the city, had seen Libby Prison and Castle Thunder, and that all the troops that could be spared had been sent to guard the city in the direction of the upper James and Brook Pike, and that there was no force of the enemy, save a small picket, on the Mechanicsville road. A thousand men were now selected, and, in two detachments of five hundred men each, under Lieutenant Colonel Preston, First Vermont, and Major ——, First Maine, were to enter the city by the Mechanicsville road, overpower the small force about the prisons, liberate our men, and then fall back upon the main force, which was to be within

General Kilpatrick shelling the city of Richmond

supporting distance.

This well devised plan, which must have been a success, was about to be undertaken, when the rebel General Hampton, with a large force of infantry and cavalry, furiously attacked our camp with musketry and artillery, and obliged the leader of the expedition to abandon all hopes of entering the city. For several hours, the desperate and confused fight continued. The enemy was finally repulsed, however, and our exhausted soldiers moved to Old Church. Here the general remained in camp all day, waiting for the return of different detachments sent out.

All came in save Dahlgren, and, finally, hearing that he had crossed the Pamunkey, and was moving to Gloucester Point, Kilpatrick slowly moved towards Yorktown, reaching that point in safety, having been five days on the march.

Colonel Dahlgren failed to accomplish the task assigned him, in consequence of the treachery of a guide, who, for his perfidy, suffered a traitor's death.

Nothing now was left for Dahlgren to do but form a junction with his general.

Rapidly he proceeded in the direction of Richmond, hoping to be in time to assist in the attack. He arrived, however, too late. All day, however, he skirmished with the enemy, and was within a few miles of Kilpatrick when the fight took place between Hampton and the former.

In the darkness of that night, with about one hundred men, Dahlgren, with Cooks, became separated from his main force. This, under Captain Mitchell, Second New York Cavalry, safely reached the main column.

Dahlgren and Cooks crossed the Pamunkey, and afterwards the Matapony, and, step by step, gallantly fought their way to a point three miles from King and Queen Court House.

And here occurred one of the most cowardly as well as cruel acts that ever disgraced any nation or any people, and that which will ever stand forth a black spot upon the history of Virginia and of the once boasted chivalry of the South.

Here Dahlgren's little band of heroic men, whose fortitude and gallantry should have excited admiration, even in the breasts of their cruel foes, were surrounded by citizens and soldiers—Dahlgren, with many of his men, cowardly murdered, and the remainder, all save seventeen out of eighty-nine, were relentlessly hunted down and some fearfully mangled and killed by bloodhounds, and the rest taken prisoners.

Colonel Dahlgren's body was stripped of his clothing, while yet alive, his little finger was severed from his hand to secure a diamond ring, the present of a near and dear friend. His body was buried in the middle of the road, as suicides were of old. It was afterwards taken up and carried to Richmond, the alleged reason being to identify it as the body upon which (to fire the Southern heart) it was falsely asserted certain orders and papers were found, containing directions to kill Jeff. Davis and cabinet, and burn the city of Richmond.

The body of this brave boy, who fell in so holy a cause, now sleeps in an unknown grave. His cruel death, and the ignominy heaped upon his lifeless body by the traitors of the South, meant to disgrace him, has only made his memory immortal, and the name of *Dahlgren* has since rung forth on many victorious fields, the battle-cry of Kilpatrick and his men. His fall, and the treatment of the brave Lieutenant-Colonel Cooks, and his five officers, have been more than avenged.

The dark, broad track of desolation that now alone remains to mark the wild ride of Kilpatrick through the State of Georgia, which we shall soon describe, and the bloody track yet to be made, will cause the terrified citizens of Virginia to meet him at the borders and beg for mercy. The spirit of Dahlgren will, indeed, have been amply avenged.

DEATH OF COLONEL DAHLGREN

CHAPTER 8

General Kilpatrick Joins Sherman

General Kilpatrick returned to his command with at least the proud satisfaction of having done all in the power of man to accomplish a noble end. That he failed was beyond human foresight to prevent, and his command, in greeting his return, felt proud of his efforts, perhaps as much as if success had crowned them; for,

> *Who does the best his circumstances allow,*
> *Does well, acts nobly; angels could no more.*

The celebrity of this grand ride will be referred to with pride as long as the American Republic cherishes the grand principles of liberty. With the command, he remained till ordered to report to Major-General Sherman, commanding the military division of the Mississippi.

In this place, events were preparing that made his services important. The mighty army that had triumphantly beaten back the foe on the field, under able leaders, now driving all before them, was the army which had covered itself with renown in the many hard-fought battles that were to dispute the advance of the Union forces between Nashville and Chattanooga. The latter place ours, the army fought its way under Sherman with great success, and the rebels were defeated in every instance, placing that great general in a prominent point of view before the nation, and sending his fame throughout the world. It was such a man as General Kilpatrick that was wanted at the time such a series of movements by cavalry were required as might insure success.

But the general who had been so widely known as a cavalry leader in the Army of the Potomac, and who therefore stood so high in the estimation of all, was now about to break up the much-loved associations of so long a period of friendship and kindly feeling, and the mutual endearments which continued associations in weal and woe produce; with these the word of parting was one of deep mutual regret. He parted with them, however, and set out, in pursuance of his order, with the firm resolve to do as he had done—strictly perform his duty to his country, and aid, with all his ability and experience, the great chief who now was making history so rapidly and doing so much to crush out the rebellion.

The general reported at Nashville, Tennessee, and was assigned to a cavalry command, and in the front, where fighting was to be done. He had not long to wait. Several severe skirmishes with the enemy were successful, and the officers and men soon began to find they had a general at their head who knew how to lead them on to victory.

He began to animate them all with the same spirit he infused into the cavalry he commanded in the army he had left.

When the grand armies under Sherman moved, Kilpatrick led the advance, with that portion of the army under General Hooker. He crossed Taylor's Ridge, driving the enemy's cavalry back to Buzzard Roost, through Snake Creek Gap, and opened up communications at Villenue with Major-General McPherson, commanding the Army of the Tennessee. At the request of that officer, he was directed by the general-in-chief to co-operate with the army of the Tennessee in its movement on Resaca, through Snake Creek Gap.

Here he made several bold reconnoissances, and finally, when General Sherman made his grand move on Resaca, General Kilpatrick again led the advance. Every soldier of the army who saw that splendid command pass out on the morning of that day could tell, by the determined looks of the men, that bold, daring deeds would soon be done. The general was never known to look so full of fight as on that day, while, dashing to the front, with his banner proudly waving to the breeze and his splendid staff about him, he passed his warm though newmade friend, the gallant Major-General Logan, Each touched his hat to the other, and Logan cried: "Give them h—ll, Kilpatrick." "Where are you going to, General?"

He replied, "No skirmishing today; but sabre charges alone shall be made."

A mile further on, and the foe was met. The Tenth Ohio was ordered to draw sabres and charge. Gallantly the order was obeyed. The enemy broke, and never ceased their flight till they met the rebel infantry advancing to their support. Kilpatrick had been directed to

General Kilpatrick wounded at Resaca

drive the enemy from the cross-roads about a mile and a half from Resaca. He directed Colonel Smith, commanding one of his brigades, to charge and drive the enemy from the crossroads. The charge was made, but our men fell back before the heavy force that met them. The general rode on the field and met his troops falling back before the rebel infantry now advancing. Ordering up a fresh brigade, he rallied the troops, and in one headlong charge rode upon the rebel infantry. The enemy was driven back, the important point gained and held, and the work assigned to the cavalry was successfully accomplished.

We have thus seen, the usual success attended this gallant commander on these fields of glory as well as in Virginia, and the trying scenes he passed through in the Army of the Potomac.

In this last wild charge, so grand and so successful, he who was the life and spirit of the cavalry was borne fainting from the field, desperately wounded by a rifle-ball, which entered at the groin, and, wonderfully escaping the large vessels, made its exit at the hip.

The same officers and men that an hour before had gayly waved him on, now sadly, sorrowfully gazed on his pale face and bloodstained garments, as he was borne to the rear in an ambulance.

Colonel Murray now assumed command, which he continued to hold about a fortnight, when he was succeeded by Colonel Lowe, who held it all the long months of the illness and convalescence of the general Nothing of importance was done by the cavalry in the meantime, and the command lay at Cartersville, Georgia.

On the thirteenth day Resaca fell, and Sherman's grand army swept on till the Chattahoochee was crossed and Atlanta invested.

General Kilpatrick had not yet entirely recovered, and was still walking on crutches, when, at his beautiful cottage on the Hudson, he read in the daily papers that Atlanta must fall in a few days. Despite the warning of his skilful surgeon, through whose exertions his wound was rapidly healing, and notwithstanding the entreaties of friends, he crossed the river, and the first train that passed carried with it the young general, impatient for the field.

All along, at the principal towns on the line of railroad, from West Point to Cincinnati, he was surrounded and welcomed by his friends, and in a few days, had reached his command at Cartersville, and marched rapidly for the front. He himself, yet unable to ride on horseback, rode in a carriage fitted up for him by his command. He reached the Chattahoochee, and took up his quarters at Sand Town.

Here, by the directions of the general-in-chief, he was busily engaged in organising and fitting out a cavalry force for an expedition in the rear of the rebel army. Many miles of the Augusta railroad had already been destroyed, and the West Point railroad had been struck at several places, a few days previously, by General Kilpatrick, on his first arrival at this point. Consequently, the rebels had but one railroad running from Macon to Atlanta over which to bring their stores, of which, it was well known, they had but twenty days' supply on hand. If these could be destroyed, the enemy would be forced to evacuate Atlanta.

General Kilpatrick was instructed to make the attempt. With two divisions of cavalry and eight pieces of artillery, numbering in all four thousand men, he left his camp at Sand Town, just as night set in, broke through the rebel cavalry lines near Fairburn, crossed the West Point railroad, and at 4 p.m, of the next day, after most severe fighting, reached the Atlanta and Macon Railroad, and occupied the place. Here, for several hours, nearly his entire command was busily engaged tearing up and destroying the railroad track and burning public property.

At 11 p.m. the enemy made a furious attack on the troops with infantry and cavalry, and forced them to cease the destruction of the road, and take up their arms for battle. The enemy was repulsed; but he now occupied a position between the general and the direction in which he wished to go. Not knowing the strength of the enemy, he left their front, and made a rapid detour in the direction of McDonough, hoping to strike the railroad farther down, and thus to place the enemy in his rear before he should be aware of his movement. But the enemy, marching on interior lines, was enabled to meet him at Lovejoy's Station. And here a most desperate battle ensued, and at one time the enemy had completely surrounded Kilpatrick, with infantry, cavalry, and artillery, and relying on the vast number they had brought against him, confidently expected to capture his entire command.

But they had laboured under a great mistake. He determined to cut his way out. He massed his men in six columns: Colonel Minty's Brigade, First Division, had the right; Colonel Murray's Brigade, Second Division, had the left of the first line of columns; Colonels Long and Jones' Brigades held the rear, while our eight pieces of artillery were rapidly firing upon the enemy.

The charge was sounded, and our men rode over the rebel barricades, sabering the men in the rear, capturing four pieces of artillery and three battle-flags, and a large number of prisoners.

After charging over the enemy, the general reformed his brigades and divisions, and fell slowly back towards McDonough's, severely repulsing such attacks as were made upon his rear. He crossed Cotton Indian River and South River the following morning, and returned to our lines at Decatur, having made a complete circuit of the rebel army.

This was a most daring as well as successful raid, and the information it gave the general-in-chief enabled him to make that great flank movement to the rear of the rebel army, giving us Atlanta, the great crowning act of Sherman's splendid campaign.

In this flank movement, with which the world is familiar, the cavalry under General Kilpatrick operated in front and on the flank of the Army of the Tennessee, Major-General Howard commanding, and was greatly distinguished for its gallant conduct during the entire movement.

After the fall of Atlanta, our army once more settled down to rest, and the cavalry took up its position on its flanks. Nothing now occurred worthy of notice, till Hood, the rebel general, made his reckless movement to flank Sherman out of Atlanta, when the cavalry kept an eye upon his motions, and had several severe skirmishes with the enemy.

The Second Division, Colonel Minty, had a severe engagement with the enemy's cavalry near Grove, gaining a complete success, and capturing two pieces of artillery. General Sherman, who had closely followed the enemy, and delayed his march until Major-General Thomas had ample time to collect and organise a force sufficient to meet him, returned to Borne, and commenced the organisation of that army which has since travelled three hundred miles through the very heart of Georgia, and finally occupied her capital city, Savannah.

The preparations for this important expedition were now making with great rapidity, and a review was made by General Kilpatrick of the fine troops composing his command. He expressed himself much pleased with the discipline of the men, and the restraint in which they were held by the gallant officers who commanded them.

Some days after, a review of the cavalry was again made by General Sherman, who spoke in the highest terms of the manner in which the troops performed their evolutions, and was known to declare, that with their help, and that of their gallant leader, he had no doubt of being able successfully to carry out the immense enterprise on which he was now about to enter. The men looked well, and were in high spirits, and their appearance on the field was one of imposing magnificence. That their bravery was equal to any emergency, and that the fortune of their general was in the ascendant, we shall find as we proceed to trace their course, step by step, from Marietta to Savannah, the great city of the South.

CHAPTER 9

Battle at East Macon

On the 30th day of October, 1864, General Kilpatrick, having received instructions from General Sherman, who commanded the military division of the Mississippi, made, at Marietta, Georgia, a concentration of the division under his command. He lost no time in fitting it out for a long and rapid march through the enemy's country; and for a matter of such moment, only a few days being given, his time was busily occupied in making such arrangements as were necessary at the very shortest notice.

There was plenty of work on hand. Horses had to be obtained, as many of his men were dismounted, or had animals totally unfit for the toils of a severe campaign; equipments were wanted; arms and clothing were needed; and a thousand other things by way of preparation against need, which might be felt where the demand for articles could meet no supply. It was necessary to call in regiments and detachments, which the requirements of the service had somewhat widely separated.

By the dint of labour and perseverance on the part of the general and all his officers, the entire command was ready for the field in little more than one week; and several regiments being added, the entire command was organised into two brigades of two thousand five hundred men each, forming, for its number, one of the best cavalry commands ever sent out on an expedition. The First Brigade, under command of Colonel Murray, consisted of the Ninth Pennsylvania Cavalry (Colonel Jordan), Fifth Kentucky Cavalry (Colonel Baldwin), Third Kentucky Cavalry (Lieutenant-Colonel King), Second Kentucky Cavalry (Captain Foreman), and Tenth Wisconsin Light Artillery, commanded by Captain Beebe.

The Second Brigade, commanded by Colonel Atkins, consisted of his own regiment, Ninety-Second Illinois Mounted Infantry (Lieutenant-Colonel Van Buskirk), Tenth Ohio Cavalry (Lieutenant-Colonel Sanderson), Fifth Ohio Cavalry (Colonel Heath), Ninth Ohio Cavalry (Colonel Hamilton), Ninth Michigan Cavalry (Colonel Acker), and First Ohio Cavalry Squadron, commanded by Captain Dazel.

The officers of the Division were invited to spend a social evening at Division Headquarters, where they enjoyed a pleasant hour in company with their leader, and had their patriotism inflamed by one of his eloquent speeches, in which he set forth the object of the anticipated expedition in such glowing words as did much to produce an *esprit de corps* and that concert of action, so important in military matters.

The morning of the fourteenth day of November is memorable as the date of breaking up the encampment at Marietta, Georgia. The night previous the numerous fires along the line of railroad indicated with what thoroughness it had been destroyed; and the lurid glare of burning houses lit up the midnight sky, and showed that the Rubicon was crossed. The entire force, consisting of five thousand five hundred men, all effective, and six pieces of artillery, marched the entire day, and having reached Atlanta, bivouacked for the night. The strong fortifications of this place, the numerous lines of earthworks seen on the march, the trees bearing the traces of bullets or broken with shot and shell, the desolate or destroyed habitations, and the numerous graves, all told the tale of war's dreadful havoc, and the cost to our troops of every foot of ground from which they had driven the retiring foe.

Here the plan of the expedition unfolded the intentions of the general-in-chief. The command was to march to Milledgeville, the capital of the State, and move on the right of the Army of the Tennessee, the right wing of the army. A feigned movement was to be made on Forsyth, and after crossing the Ocmulgee River a feint was to be made of attacking Macon, the Georgia and Central Railroad to be struck as near Macon as possible, and to fall back in the direction of Gordon, thoroughly destroying the railroad General Kilpatrick was to wait till the infantry came up, and report to the general-in-chief at Milledgeville.

In accordance with these instructions, which were to be carried out in seven days, Kilpatrick left Atlanta November 15th, and, having crossed Flint River, occupied Jonesboro'. It was reported that part of General Wheeler's cavalry, and the Georgia militia, under command of General Cobb, were at Lovejoy Station. The next morning the advance of Wheeler's cavalry was met and repulsed, and he was found in line of battle in the old rebel fortifications thrown up by the army of General Hood, on its retreat from Jonesboro' some time previous. Their works were charged and carried by the troops under Colonel Murray, who recaptured two three-inch rifled guns lost by General Stoneman, killing and wounding a large number of the enemy, and forcing them, in great confusion, to retreat to Bear Creek Station.

Here Wheeler attempted a halt, with the intention of making a stand; but Colonel Atkins having now come up, charged him vigorously with the Tenth Ohio Cavalry, broke his line, and forced him, with the Georgia militia, from the field, till he halted fourteen miles distant, at the town of Griffin.

Kilpatrick having got rid of the enemy for the time being, and intent on destroying as much rebel property as possible, and particularly cotton, cotton-gins, and other property of great value to the bogus Confederacy, divided his command, and marched his troops on two roads. Having made a feint as if Forsyth was his object, and assuming that the enemy was deceived, he moved rapidly to Planters' Factory, and crossing the Ocmulgee, reached Clinton on the 17th of November, at which place he learned that part of Wheeler's force had crossed the river near Macon, and now confronted him.

Advancing towards Macon, he met and repulsed Wheeler's cavalry, and driving him across Walnut Greek, assaulted and carried a portion of their works, old Fort Hawkins, about East Macon. The fighting was done by the Tenth Ohio Cavalry and Ninety-Second Illinois Mounted Infantry, these regiments having the advance, and the fighting and bravery displayed called forth praise from their leader. The enemy and skill of Colonel Atkins, commanding the Second Brigade, are much commended by his chief

The command encamped for the night on the railroad and the road leading from Macon to Milledgeville; Walnut Creek was picketed, and the entire night was spent in destroying the railroad, by a force of one-third the whole command. Already Captain Ladd, with a detachment of the Ninth Michigan Cavalry, had reached the railroad at Griswold Station, and captured thirteen cars, freighted with engines, driving-wheels, and wheels and springs. The station, a pistol and a soap and candle factory were destroyed or burned.

In a battle which took place next day at Griswold Station, every attack of the enemy, by infantry and cavalry, was repulsed. A few days later Wheeler advanced with his entire cavalry corps, in addition to which he had three brigades of infantry, and confident in his strength he attacked the Union pickets, which he drove in, as also the skirmish line. But his efforts were in vain, for he was finally checked and driven back by the Ninth Pennsylvania Cavalry, under Colonel Jordan, and the Fifth Kentucky, commanded by Colonel Baldwin.

The principal weapon used in this engagement was the sabre. The infantry, under General Walcot, having come up, drove the enemy beyond Griswold Station. On the same day Colonel Atkins, commanding Second Brigade, had a severe engagement with the enemy on the road leading from Macon to Milledgeville, arid kept him from molesting our trains, then on the road between Clinton and Gordon.

The command had now reached Milledgeville, the capital of the State, and at this place rested a few hours, during which supplies were obtained This town is pleasantly situated on the Oconee River, and is a place of some importance. The Legislature had been in session here a short time before, and left everything in confusion. Books, official papers, bills before the Legislature, the recent message of Governor Brown, and a host of curious papers, were scattered through the rooms of the capitol. The capitol building was situated near the arsenal, and when the magazine in the latter was blown up shared the same fate. It was a matter of some regret, perhaps, to destroy an edifice so stately, but, no doubt, it was a military necessity.

General Kilpatrick, agreeable to instructions, had met the general-in-chief at Milledgeville, and was ordered to move rapidly towards Millen, and set at liberty the prisoners that were said to be confined there. Accordingly, he made a rapid movement towards Augusta, and crossing the Ogeechee River at the shoals reached the railroad at Waynesboro'. The preceding day. Captain Estes, Kilpatrick's assistant adjutant-general, in command of the advance, had destroyed part of the railway at Waynesboro', and burned a portion of the railroad bridge over Briar Creek.

The column had been attacked several times in flank during the march, and it was evidently the intention of the rebel general to harass Kilpatrick as much as possible as he advanced, to destroy him, and then he would have it all his own way with the supply trains of the army; yet no immediate signs had, up to the present, manifested an intention of any very vigorous attack. Skirmishes on the flank and rear had not been attended with any very serious result, though it was apprehended that, at some point on the march, the enemy would make a stand, and a severe battle ensue.

The command, having advanced through Waynesboro', encamped

about three miles south of it on the railroad, and remained in position. In order to completely destroy the railroad, one battalion was taken from each regiment for that purpose, and while this was being done several attacks were made upon Colonel Murray, but handsomely repulsed, and the baffled enemy rendered incapable of molesting those engaged in tearing up the track. While thus occupied the general learned, with great regret, that the prisoners confined at Millen had been removed two days previous; so, it was thus out of his power now to procure their liberation. Had they remained at Millen, it cannot be doubted but that they would have been rescued, despite all opposition on the part of the Confederate Government. The matter, however, could not now be mended

When a sufficient portion of the track had been destroyed, so as to prevent communication for a few days, the general deemed it prudent to retire to the infantry force, which lay at Louisville. With this design, he ordered Colonel Atkins, with Second Brigade, to move to the point where the Waynesboro' and Louisville roads cross each other, and there take up a position. Colonel Murray, with First Brigade, was, in the meantime, directed to move past Colonel Atkins and take up a position in his rear, and so on throughout the day, and thus withdraw from any portion of the enemy's forces that might be following them up. Owing to some misapprehension, the general and staff, together with two regiments—Eighth Indiana Cavalry (Colonel Jones), and Seventh Michigan Cavalry (Colonel Acker)—being too far separated from the rest of the command, in consequence of the too rapid march of Colonel Atkins, and being cut completely off, were partly surrounded by the enemy's cavalry.

The author will never forget the moment when an *aide* rode up, with excited looks, and sweat felling in drops from himself and horse, and announced that General Kilpatrick was cut off. The news ran through the column like electricity; the column halted and formed in line of battle, and, throwing up barricades, presented a front which told fighting was to be done, and that the enemy must break through that line before he could advance another step. Matters, however, had not come to that; the brave regiments, whose officers and men deserve and obtained the highest commendation, officially, by splendid fighting broke the enemy's lines, and beating them back .at every point he attacked, fell slowly back till the main column was reached.

The march now continued, and after crossing Buckhead Creek, burned the bridge, and halted two miles distant for the purpose of resting their jaded horses. It was here ascertained that Wheeler was crossing the creek with his entire force.

The general now determined to give him a repulse he would not soon forget, and having taken up a strong position, with flank well thrown to the rear, he threw up barricades, which were scarcely completed when the enemy came rushing on; a few minutes later there occurred one of the most desperate cavalry charges that can well be imagined, but with slight loss to the Union forces; the enemy met a severe repulse at all points, and the fight terminated.

No attempts were now made on the part of the enemy to annoy the march the balance of the day. The command marched a few miles forward, encamping in a place where forage was plenty and could easily be obtained.

The losses sustained by the command were inconsiderable, considering there was continuous fighting for three days and nights. Through scouts, prisoners, and deserters it was ascertained pretty clearly that the enemy's losses in killed and wounded amounted to six hundred.

Next day the left wing of our army was reached at Louisville, where a rest of several days, the first on the march, recruited the tired soldiers and their horses, which were now almost worn down by hard marching day and night.

Our troops, in several columns, were now marching on Millen, and in order to cover their movements, the cavalry command, on the second day of December, moved on the Waynesboro' road, in advance of a division of infantry, commanded by General Baird. Colonel Baldwin, with the Fifth Kentucky. Cavalry, and Colonel Jones, with the Eighth Indiana Cavalry, encountered a small body of the enemy, and after a brisk skirmish put them to flight.

The infantry now arrived, and on reaching Rocky Creek, and a considerable force of the enemy being found on the opposite side, a force of cavalry and infantry crossed at the same time, and charging, drove the enemy into rapid retreat towards Waynesboro' and Augusta, the cavalry following up in hot pursuit.

The command then moved on to Thomas Station, and an encampment was made for the night. General Baird's command was now busily employed in destroying the railroad, and in accomplishing this design were deployed along the track for miles. Kilpatrick made such a disposition of his men as to protect Baird's troops in their work; while these forces were thus engaged, Wheeler, who had encamped between Waynesboro' and Brier Creek, moved early in the evening with part of his command to Waynesboro'. He made a fierce attack on one of Colonel Atkins's regiments, encamped on the railroad three miles from Waynesboro', to the south of the town. There was little difficulty in repulsing this and similar attacks made during the night.

General Kilpatrick had received instructions from the general-in-chief to make a reconnaissance in force towards Waynesboro', and fight Wheeler wherever he might encounter him. Accordingly, he issued his orders to brigade commanders to "strip for a fight," and everything that would incommode his command to be sent to the rear, in order that in the morning the cavalry, unimpeded in meeting the enemy, would be in a situation to defeat and rout the rebel cavalry encamped at Waynesboro'.

CHAPTER 10

Battle of Waynesboro'

The following morning Kilpatrick moved his forces, and the advance was led by Colonel Atkins, Second Brigade. The enemy's skirmish line was encountered, and, after a few minutes of sharp skirmishing, were driven in and forced to retire to their main body. The enemy's lines were made up of dismounted cavalry, strongly posted behind long lines of barricades, having the flanks well extended to the rear. Colonel Atkins was ordered to take the barricades; but the enemy being somewhat stronger than was anticipated, the bold attack he made upon the line proved a failure.

A second attack was made. The Ninety-Second Illinois Mounted Infantry dismounted; the Tenth Ohio Cavalry and Ninth Michigan Cavalry, in columns of fours by battalion, sent in on the right, and the Ninth Ohio Cavalry placed in the same manner on the left also. On the left, the Tenth Wisconsin Battery, commanded by Captain Beebe, was brought up to within six hundred yards of the barricades, and, opening an effective fire, forced the enemy's artillery (five pieces in all) to withdraw from the contest. This was the favourable moment for attack. Accordingly, the charge was sounded, and the whole line, in magnificent order, advanced without a moment's halt, took the barricades, and the enemy was forced to retire.

After falling back some hundred yards, he made several counter-charges to check our rapid advance, so as to enable him to relieve his dismounted men; and he was, at one time, almost successful, when he was attacked in flank by Colonel Heath, with Fifth Ohio Cavalry, which had been sent out on our right. The enemy yielded to this charge, gave way, and beaten at all points, rapidly fell back to the town of Waynesboro', where he took up a new position.

In this position, he was strongly posted within a second line of barricades, protected with artillery, having his flanks, as before, so far extended that any attempt at turning them was of no avail.

The general then determined to break his centre, and ordered Colonel Murray, who had the advance, to make his dispositions accordingly, which was immediately done. The Eighth Indiana Cavalry, commanded by Colonel Jones, was at once dismounted and sent forward as skirmishers; the Ninth Pennsylvania Cavalry, commanded by Colonel Jordan, held the left in columns of four by battalion; the Third Kentucky Cavalry, commanded by Lieutenant-Colonel King, had the centre, while Colonel Baldwin, with the Fifth Kentucky Cavalry, and Captain Foreman, with Second Kentucky Cavalry, held the right.

The charge was sounded. The brave men advanced on the rebels with impetuosity, drove them out of their position, and taking possession of the town, followed up their routed forces in hot pursuit, with the Fifth Ohio, Fifth Kentucky, and a portion of the Ninth Pennsylvania Cavalry.

The pursuit continued to Brier Creek, eight miles distant from the place where the enemy had first been attacked. The railroad bridge was burned, and the railroad destroyed by tearing up and burning the track. The Union forces then marched to Alexander, and encamped for the night.

The enemy, under Wheeler, consisted of four divisions and two independent brigades, and the author has occasion to know, from the acknowledgment of the rebels themselves, that the rout was a complete one. Wheeler, after this, permitted our cavalry, unmolested, to continue its march, and was never after able to rally his shattered columns, which were totally demoralised. General Kilpatrick, in his official report of the expedition, says:

> The men of my command fought most bravely throughout this day, and it is impossible to single out from among the officers, individual cases of gallantry, where all did so well. My casualties on this day, as well as on all others, will be found on a separate report accompanying this. Judging from the enemy's killed and wounded, left on the field, his loss must have been severe, as upwards of two hundred left in our hands were wounded by the sabre alone.

> *Dec. 5.*—We marched from Alexander to Jacksonboro' covering the rear of the Fourteenth Army Corps.

> *Dec. 6.*—Colonel Murray, with First Brigade, marched to

Springfield, moving in the rear of the Twentieth Army Corps. The Second Brigade, Colonel Atkins, moved to Hudson's Ferry.

Dec. 7.—When near Sister's Ferry, the Ninth Michigan Cavalry, Colonel Acker, acting as rear guard to the Second Brigade, received and repulsed an attack of Ferguson's Cavalry.

Dec. 8.—The Second Brigade crossed Ebenezer Creek, and the whole command united on the Monteith road, tea miles from Springfield. From this point the command moved in the rear of the Seventeenth Army Corps, detachments covering the rear of several Army Corps, till the army reached the rebel lines, and commenced the investment of Savannah.

Dec. 12.—My command crossed the Ogeechee and Conoochee, and marched to attack and capture Fort McAllister. Striking distance had already been reached, a reconnaissance made, all requisite information gained, when, in accordance with the expressed wish of the general-in-chief, I abandoned my design of attack, and with my command moved to reconnoitre St. Catherine's Sound, and open up our communication with our fleet. This was accomplished before 11 o'clock, a. m. The same day Fort McAllister fell.

Dec. 15.—The command returned to the vicinity of King's Bridge and went into camp, picketing the Conoochee and country in direction of Altamaha River.

Dec. 17.—Colonel Atkins, with upwards of two thousand men of my command, moved in conjunction with a division of infantry under General Mower, to destroy a portion of the Gulf Railroad, and, if possible, the railroad bridge over the Altamaha. Difficult approaches, and a strong force of the enemy, which could not be dislodged, prevented the accomplishment of the latter. The railroad, however, was very thoroughly destroyed, and the command returned to camp.

Dec. 21.—The enemy evacuated Savannah, the army occupied the city, and the operations of the cavalry closed.

In carrying out the orders of the commander-in-chief, and in making the diversions in them indicated, some mistakes may have been made, yet I believe that the principal operations and diversions required of the cavalry have been throughout the march successfully accomplished. Certainly, it is a fact, that not once has the enemy's cavalry been able to reach the train or flank of one of our infantry columns. We have three times crossed from left to right, and right to left, in front of our army, and have marched upwards of five hundred and forty-one miles since the 14th day of November, and have destroyed fourteen hundred and four bales of cotton, two hundred and seventy-one cotton-gins, and much other valuable property; have captured two throe-inch rifled guns, and have them now in use; captured and destroyed eight hundred and sixty-three stands of small arms, and killed, wounded, and disabled not less than fifteen hundred of the enemy.

We have lost four officers killed, six wounded, and two missing; thirty-four men killed, ono hundred and fifty-three wounded, and one hundred and sixty-six missing.

Before closing my remarks, I desire to make favourable mention of my brigade commanders, Colonels Murray and Atkins. Both have, at all times, faithfully and ably performed the responsible duties that have devolved upon them. Always on duty, attentive to orders, energetic, skilful, and brave; both at educated, gentlemanly, and accomplished cavalry officers. Both merit promotion.

Colonel Sanderson and his regiment. Tenth Ohio Cavalry, at East Macon; Colonel Acker, and his regiment, Ninth Michigan Cavalry; Colonel Jones, and his regiment, Eighth Indiana Cavalry, when cut off and surrounded near Waynesboro'; Colonel Heath, and his regiment, Fifth Ohio, at Buckhead Creek; the Ninety-Second Illinois Mounted Infantry, Lieutenant-Colonel Van Buskirk; Ninth Pennsylvania Cavalry, Colonel Jordan; Third Kentucky Cavalry, Lieutenant-Colonel King; Tenth Ohio, Fifth Ohio, and Ninth Michigan Cavalry, at Waynesboro', December 4th, have all, at the various places mentioned, behaved most handsomely, and attracted my special attention.

The Second Kentucky Cavalry, Captain Foreman, although but a detachment, at Buckhead Creek, and at Waynesboro', did the duty of a regiment, and deserve the highest praise.

Captain Beebe, commanding artillery, and his lieutenants, Stetson, Fowler, and Clark, have performed their duty well, and to the satisfaction of their immediate commanders.

I cannot speak too highly of the conduct of my staff. Through the exertions of Captain Dunbar, A. Q. M., and Captain Brookfield, C. S., my command has always been well supplied. Dr.

Wise, Surgeon-in-Chief of Division; Captains Brink, A. A. J. Guil, and Day, provost-marshals; and my *aides*, Captain Hayes, and Lieutenants Hollingsworth, Oliver, and Fuller, have, each in his respective place, more than fulfilled my expectation.

Captain Estes, my assistant adjutant-general, deserves special notice, not only for the faithful discharge of his eminent duties, but for his reckless daring and invaluable assistance in every skirmish and engagement. This officer deserves, and I earnestly hope, that he may be promoted.

Accompanying this report will be found a nominal list of killed, wounded, and missing; also, provost-marshal's statement of captures, and property destroyed. I enclose the reports of my brigade and regimental commanders, which I respectfully request may be taken as part of this my official report.

General Kilpatrick was accompanied during the campaign by his young nephew, W, Judson Kilpatrick, a promising youth of fourteen, and a *hero* in the New York papers, in which his bravery has been extolled. His uncle, anxious for his well-being and future prospects, attends to his recitations. But this young scion of the Kilpatrick stock is rather lively, and not particularly ambitious in his studies.

The manner in which the services of General Kilpatrick were estimated, and the honour gained by the officers and men under his command, cannot be better evinced than in the following letter from the general-in-chief, received on New Year's Day, 1865:

Headquarters, Military Division of the Mississippi
In the field of Savannah, Ga.
December 29, 1864

Brigadier-General Judson Kilpatrick,
Commanding Cavalry Division, Army of Georgia:
General: I read with pleasure your report, just received, as well as those of your brigade commanders. I beg to assure you that the operations of the cavalry have been skilful and eminently successful. As you correctly state in your report, you handsomely feigned on Forsyth and Macon, and afterwards did all that was possible towards the rescue of our prisoners at Millen, which failed simply because our prisoners were not there. And I will here state, that you may have it on my signature that you acted wisely and well in drawing back from Wheeler to Louisville, as I had instructed you not to risk your cavalry command.

And subsequently, at Thomas' Station, Waynesboro', and Brier Greek, you whipped a superior cavalry force, and took from Wheeler all chance of boasting over you.

But the fact that to you, in a great measure, we owe the march of four strong infantry columns, with heavy trains and wagons, over three hundred miles through an enemy's country, without the loss of a single wagon, and without the annoyance of cavalry dashes on our flanks, is honour enough for any cavalry commander.

I will retain your report for a few days, that I may, in my own report, use some of your statistics, and then will forward it to the War Department, when I will indorse your recommendations, and make such others as I may consider necessary and proper.

> I am truly,
> > Your friend,

(Signed)   W. T. Sherman
Major-General Comd'g

The following "Poem," denominated "*Kilpatrick*," is copied from one of the public journals, and appeared about this time, but seems to have been written some time previously, and will show that the poet's pen was used to perpetuate the glories of a success not ephemeral, but for the country's sake permanent. The candid reader may form his own opinion about it; the writer was, doubtless, one of the general's old companions:

KILPATRICK.

Kilpatrick! friend, so young, and yet so famed,
In every clime and every language named;
I saw thee, when a schoolboy, watch the wave
The lovely valley of the Walkill lave;
But little thought that thine would be the arm.
So slight, so soft, to shield the State from harm;
I knew thee when the nation's care and pride
Upon the eaglet eyrie close beside
The cliff-bound river, whence have soared with thee.
Full fledged, the champions of the free.

But little thought that mild blue eye of thine
Would flash dismay in friends of auld lang syne.
And thou fierce squadrons lead on dread forays

Through lands and homes, we loved in other days,
And wear so soon the longed-for silver star
That blazes ever in the front of war,
Its glories mingling with the trophies won
By Randall and our Pennington.

God bless thee for thy pertinacity,
Thy dash and thy sublime audacity,
That, like a very eagle, made thee dare
To pounce upon the lion in his lair.
And beat, with dreadful beak, his wondering eyes,
Then soar unruffled back to Northern skies.
Hail, knight without reproach or fear, all hail!
A nation for thy lost ones lifts her wail,
And proudly claims thee for her own today.
Wife—child, are gone; thy country lives alway:
Press on! press on! Atlanta is before.
Heed not the fruit she flings as flung of yore:
That lover only wins the maiden prize
Who to the golden apples shuts his eyes.
Heed not the wound, it still will let thee lead,
Though blood is trickling down thy charging steed.

Charge on! charge on! The Georgian pines are bare,
Trust in thy star, and send them flying there;
Make clear the way the army yet shall go.
And shroud its motions from the baffled foe;
Keep on thy road, the wild morass is wide.
Our hearts are with thee, Kil., whatever betide.
Haste on! a world expectant waits for thee!
Ride on! thou gallant raider, to the sea!
We wait, we hear; thy name rings out the most,
And will, with his, the leader of the host.
Hail! risen Ney! uutouched by rivalry.
Charge on! charge on! with all thy cavalry!

Hark, 'tis the bugle sound! the charge is made.
The Flint is crossed, fierce squadrons are arrayed;
Here frowning earth-works rise, the foe to shield
That in them swarm, and on the extended field
'Tis Lovejoy's Station's glorious scene is laid,
Where gallant Murray hurls his bold brigade.

And Wheeler with his horsemen o'er the plain
In wild confusion drives, and slacks the rein;
The foe his wounded leaves, and leaves his slain—
And by the furious charge of Atkins driven,
A close pursuit his shattered force is given.
What though at Millen captives mourn in vain
The grand, the bold design to break their chain,
Yet Macon's, Griswold's fight beheld thy force,
Thy charge resistless; and the rebel horse
Thy matchless might confess in grief and sorrow,
While o'er their barricades rush at Waynesboro'
Thy furious steed, thy staff, while in the air
And o'er the field unfurled thy banner fair—
With thy loved name inscribed, fair Alice, lost!—
Now tells the rebel and the conquering host
The victor chief has highest honours won.
By Sherman sounded wide beneath the sun!

CHAPTER 11

Promoted to Major-General

The cavalry arm of the service has ever been our pride. We have watched its brilliant course, from the first daring charge made by Tompkins and his regulars through the streets of Fairfax Court-House in 1861, and its glorious achievements on the broad plains of Brandy Station, Beverly Ford, Aldie, Hanover, Pennsylvania, Kilpatrick's and Grierson's daring raids—which rival their great opponents, Jeb. Stuart, Morgan, Forrest, and Wheeler—up to the magnificent ride by General Kilpatrick and his six thousand horsemen through the heart of Georgia.

We have read and admired, in days gone by, Richard *Coeur de Lion's* deeds of daring, the splendid contests on the plains of Palestine, Murat's wild charges and splendid career, as well as those of our own Marion and Light Horse Harry Lee, of Revolutionary fame; and the renowned charge of *six hundred* in the Crimea, at Balaklava But not one nor all of these excel, or even rival, the deeds of fame achieved by our own great cavalry generals, as seen by Kilpatrick's famous raids in the East, Grierson's in the West, Pleasanton's victories in Virginia, Kilpatrick's and Custer's in Pennsylvania, and Torbert's in the Shenandoah Valley, who rival in greatness and splendor the most celebrated European cavalry heroes immortalized by poet's or historian's pen.

The author has long intended to write not only a partial but full and complete history of our cavalry; and this, at a future period, may be accomplished, and a particular description of all the *res gestae* of our eminent cavalry commanders, living and departed, obtain the place to which a grateful country acknowledges them entitled, for it is the memory of such the historian loves to perpetuate.

Much could be said, too, of the brave brigade commanders, who are, many of them, known to be worthy of all praise, and capable of being promoted to high rank. And do not our regimental commanders claim the thanks of their superiors and inferiors in rank alike? The field officers, always exposed on the battlefield—majors, captains, lieutenants—all fit to rise up and fill any place made vacant.

One rank in the service demands a word—the non-commissioned officers—men who, by capacity, knowledge of tactics, soldierly bearing and uniform good conduct, have greatly, to the author's knowledge, added to the efficiency of the cavalry command, and at all times have proved, that when a vacancy occurs each regiment, nay, each company, can procure fit successors to stand forward and fill up the gap made by shot or shell, disease or death. The sergeant is the man who leads out his men and relieves guard—on whom, in camp, on the bivouac, on picket or on the skirmish line, his immediate superior relies. The corporal is an important officer, and a slight mistake may be fatal to his general, who depends on him as much, or perhaps more, than on those of rank much superior. The chevrons have and do encircle stalwart arms, and great honour is due our brave non-commissioned officers.

The bulk of any army, however, is made up of privates,, or men who serve their country on the march, the bivouac, the camp, the picket, the guard, the skirmish-line, the battle-line. They endure the toils and fatigues of war—long, tedious marches, day and night. The march over, put on guard to the camp, or on picket, or to go to sleep in the cold, on the blanket, or without it, under the star-studded canopy, resting on and sleeping on their arms, till, roused at the bugle-sound, they rise from broken slumbers, and perhaps with empty stomach, to defend the assaulted barricade, hurl back the foe, charge him with enthusiastic bravery, and push the advantage into total rout.

Discipline, tactics, the military exercises, make these men able to cope with and conquer all difficulties. The author knows well the men of the cavalry command, and honours and respects the brave soldier who fights the battles of his country, and continually is found at his post in danger's hour, and obedient to the word of command.

Kilpatrick's success greatly depended on the *care* he took of his men, and the discipline they were subjected to. Their arms, equipments, clothing, subsistence, and, in a word, everything in which the welfare of the soldier is concerned, he looked into with anxious solicitude, and what was lacking he supplied as far as lay in his power. The men confided in him, and such was their reliance on, and attachment to him, he could lead them anywhere, and had only to let them know he wanted them to do such and such things, and they were done.

His success, too, was augmented by the animated and cheerful manner in which he addressed them on an emergency on the field of battle. Everyone is conversant with the pithy words, on a certain critical occasion: "Back the *Harris Light!*" "Back the Tenth New York!" "Reform your squadrons, and charge!" How soon and how well the order was executed, and with what result, we have already seen. It was thus that, ever cool and collected, bold as a lion, and prudent, not *rash*, as some misinformed persons have charged, he often turned the tide of battle, rolled it back upon the foe, till they were overthrown.

General Sherman bears witness to his ability and daring, but not this only; for that mighty warrior, one of the best judges, and who best knew, expressly states that this leader was "skilful and prudent," and "saved his command." With military men, but little value can attach to an opinion to the contrary of that expressed by so distinguished a judge as General Sherman.

Readiness of mind was another great reason why success attended him; his fertility of resources, and knowledge how to take advantage of occasions as they arose. All was prepared—all ready—the final disposition made with great care, and the possibility of failure all but excluded.

There was, too, his rare knowledge of men, and acquaintance with human nature. He knew how to put "the right man in the right place," and always kept the right sort of men about him, even to his orderly, his servant, and his cook. None more quickly than he could tell whether his horse was well groomed or not, and woe to the luckless wight that was negligent! for "a merciful man is merciful to his beast:" dumb animals ever came in for a share of his care, and, like all good cavalry officers, he was very careful of his horse, and took great pride in his trappings. Though not an epicure, but very plain in his mode of living, he is a nice judge of culinary operations; on several occasions at dinner we have observed his nice discrimination of dishes, and if not well prepared, his dissatisfaction is apparent.

Thus, even in the minor details, he is nice upon every point; the little things that many would pass over, his keen eye detected at once; and he would want, if the thing could be done, to have it done well.

Acting upon this principle, when a man was found who could do anything well, he attached him to him, and, therefore, everything done was well done, and reflected credit on the doer as well as on himself.

In all his selections, if there is any point in which he might be fastidious, it is in the selection of his staff officers. His opinion of them can be gathered from his own official report, and it is sufficient to say, they were all energetic and able young gentlemen, whom we have found it pleasant to associate with at all times. It is not too much to say, that they are gallant young fellows, ready to do whatever directed in the promptest manner, and to be depended on in any crisis,—which, to a general who was always raiding or fighting, or devising fresh schemes, was not seldom the case. I have frequently heard it said that Kilpatrick's staff did more work than any general's staff in the army.

General Kilpatrick always takes a deep interest in young men, especially those of his staff, who found in him a kind, genuine, true friend; one who felt interested in them, and gained their confidence; was consulted by them in their most important affairs, and ever found, when occasion offered, desirous of advancing their interests in every possible way.

But they seldom remain with him long. So efficient are they found to be, from the thorough training under such a master, forming their minds and characters after such a man, and naturally becoming influenced thereby, that they are soon wanted in higher positions, and promotion takes them from him, but never interrupts the friendly feeling and true affection that bound them mutually together. The grave, indeed, sometimes. separates them, but it does not, with all its gloom, do away with or impair the sentiments he cherished for their memory; of their regards for him it may be said they were perpetual, and of his for them that it was "immortal."

We have yet to find the common soldier who will speak of General Kilpatrick in any terms save of praise; and, indeed, the feeling is reciprocated. Kilpatrick loves his men. I have heard him say, on many occasions, when, true to him, some regiment or detachment gloriously charged the barricades, or stubbornly held some important post, "God bless the brave soldiers!—every one of them deserves promotion."

To show the talent for the selection of his staff, it will be sufficient to mention such names as Dahlgren and Cook, already alluded to; Hackley, the eminent surgeon and elegant gentleman, who, for two years, never left the general's side, not even in the most dangerous hour, and who well sustained the dignity of the profession, and earned the merited esteem cherished for him; Armstrong, for so long a time his able inspector-general; Whitaker, Wilson, and Northrop, those brave young men who, in the East as well as in the West, have won for themselves a most enviable reputation.

Llewellyn G. Estes, that gallant soldier from Maine who, from the very first, has been with the general, sharing every danger; who, for so many months, has been his adjutant-general, the responsible duties of which office have been so ably performed, and whose daring and usefulness on the field of battle have won for him a reputation second to no young officer in the army.

Captains Brink, Day, Hayes, Dunbar, Brookfield, and Lieutenants Lewis, Hollingsworth, and Fuller, who have, in every battle and on every occasion, proved themselves worthy of serving on the staff of a general so illustrious. Lieutenants Wedemeyer, Newton, McCrea, Oliver, and Potter, who, if not so long with the general, are no less attached, and share also his esteem and confidence; as well as his medical director, Surgeon Helm, a gentleman of scientific ability, whose professional attainments and skill are only equalled by his humanity.

We have reason to believe—in fact, to know,—that the want of success of many of our generals, and with some of those who have commanded armies, has been the result, not so much of their own want of ability, but from the fact that, in many cases, they have gathered about them an incompetent and worthless staff, who knew less of military matters than the orderly who rode in their rear and held their horses.

Point out a general who has been successful, and he will be found to have ever had about him an intelligent, accomplished, energetic staff.

Another element that gave success to General Kilpatrick was, his great tact and business talent, or "administrative ability," in which he so far excelled the most of military men as to place him, in this respect, beyond competitors; for his natural powers, in themselves quick, ready, elastic, were improved by science, study, and cultivation, and, combined with tact, rendered him preeminent and successful.

We cannot better express the patriotic ardour and steady purpose of General Kilpatrick faithfully to perform his duty, than by laying before our readers the following communication to Major-General Sherman, General-in-chief:

January 2 1865

General:

I have always felt convinced that you were satisfied with the efforts I have made to carry out your orders, and with the part my command has taken in your late important and successful operations. Bat I was not prepared for your communication, and the grateful words it contained. It was placed in my hands on New Year's Day, and I would not exchange the happiness it has given me for all the wealth in Savannah (cotton included), a New Year's gift sent by you to our worthy President.

My command has been furnished with copies, and I assure you, general, that now no task will be too difficult, no march too long, no rebel force too formidable; but with strong arms and brave hearts, proud of your recognition of our efforts in the past, we will do more, dare more than ever, to have General Sherman say, at the close of a campaign which I feel will be the beginning of the end, 'I am satisfied with my cavalry.'

On the 14th of January, 1865, Kilpatrick was made Major-General.

Chapter 12

Kilpatrick's Feints and Diversions

We Americans, like the Athenians, are a fickle, changeable people; we make a man today, and unmake him tomorrow; we place a garland of roses on his brow, while we are looking for thorns to place under his feet. A hundred victories in the past are swallowed up in one defeat, and new heroes usurp in our hearts the place of those whose past services, wounds, and glorious deeds, should have endeared them to us forever. In view of these facts, it is indeed a daring matter to risk opinions, or even attempt to write the history of a soldier whose career of usefulness and glory we hope has only just begun.

The last chapter was finished while Sherman's veteran army was resting among the cypress and pines about Savannah. The Union troops, then in occupation of that interesting old city, with its Revolutionary earthworks, its "Pulaski" monument, and various remains of the past, enjoyed a much-needed repose, and had their patriotism fired by contemplation of memorials of bygone days. Sherman passed his mighty legions in review, and as corps after corps in all the splendor of glittering arms appeared before the inhabitants, a magnificent spectacle was presented, and could not have failed to impress upon their minds the strength and power of that government against which they had dared to rebel.

It was here that preparation was made for the great campaign now about to be inaugurated. The army of Sherman was to march upon what proved one of the most successful and grand expeditions that the pen of history records. South Carolina, despite her formidable rivers, swamps, and boastful soldiery, has been traversed by our victorious army, and her capital, Columbia, and many towns, left like ruins upon the desert—desolate and pitiable.

Alas! that ever a land so favoured should, like that fair city of old,

102

be left "a place for the bittern and water-pools."

While our army is now resting from its glorious march, I shall attempt to lay before the reader in this last chapter a correct account of the part taken by Kilpatrick and his cavalry, although, in a work like this full justice cannot be done this officer or his men. The many feints and diversions, rapid and forced marches —that tireless activity without which his command, even in the immediate neighbourhood of the foe, vastly superior in numbers, would have been ruined; his resistless onsets, stubborn fight, and victory over Hampton's and Wheeler's combined forces; and the splendid fighting, mounted and on foot, side by side with our infantry, near the close of the campaign, which won for the cavalry the admiration of the entire army, deserve, not a single chapter, but a whole volume by itself.

By the 15th of January, Sherman's grand army of invasion was ready for the campaign. The troops were eager to tread the "sacred soil" of South Carolina, and hailed with joy the order that was to send them on their perilous march, fraught with so many untried dangers.

The Seventeenth and Fifteenth Corps, on the morning of the 16th of February, quietly left the city of Savannah, and, to the astonishment of the enemy, suddenly attacked and took possession of Pocotaligo Landing, S. C. This initiated the grand campaign, While the enemy were speculating as to what point General Sherman would move, the left wing, General Slocum commanding, moved to Sister's Ferry, and, after many days of incessant labour, the Savannah was ready to be crossed.

The cavalry command, under General Kilpatrick, which had up to this time been quietly resting behind the infantry, now crossed the river on a pontoon at Sister's Ferry, passed through the formidable swamp beyond, and moved rapidly on Augusta.

This movement was unknown to the enemy, and not expected, as General Howard had already pushed his column across the Salkehatchie, far on the right, indicating a movement of the whole army on Columbia *via* Branchville; so that by rapid marching Kilpatrick had reached and crossed the Salkehatchie, and occupied Barnwell, thirty miles to the left front of General Howard, and in the direction of Augusta, before the movement was discovered.

The rebel General Wheeler now left the front of the Army of the Tennessee, and moved rapidly to get in Kilpatrick's front, in order to save the railroad; but he was too late.

At 9 a.m., February 7th, Kilpatrick struck the Charleston and Augusta Railroad at Blackville, and drove Wheeler across the Edisto. The following day the entire army, save one corps, occupied the line of this important railroad from the Edisto River to Blackville, and the work of destruction commenced. Columbia was Sherman's true objective point; yet Augusta, in the opinion of the enemy, might be. Up to this time, all the bridges and crossings over the Edisto, in the direction of Columbia, were strongly guarded; but Kilpatrick's deliberate movement up the railroad, destroying in the direction of Augusta, had at last the desired effect.

He had reached Johnston's Station, five miles from Aiken, and nineteen miles from Augusta, when the enemy became alarmed for the safety of that city. Major-General Wheeler at once uncovered Columbia, and, by marching night and day, reached Aiken in advance of Kilpatrick; and, supported by the rebel General Cheatham's corps of infantry, disputed his further progress.

For two days, he skirmished with the enemy, till our various infantry columns had crossed the Edisto, and were well headed for Columbia; then suddenly leaving Wheeler's front, he crossed the Edisto, and marched to Lexington Court-House, preventing Wheeler's reaching Columbia, and forcing that general and the remainder of Hood's army to make a wide detour, in order to get in Sherman's front.

Columbia, the capital of South Carolina, fell without a struggle; and the chivalry, who had sworn to defend her honour—"drive back the ruthless, rude, brutal invaders"—and save the Confederacy, or nobly die amid her sacred altars, had cowardly fled, broken, widely scattered, baffled, and dispirited, by that splendid strategy of Sherman, which had, in a few days, laid South Carolina at the feet and mercy of the men of the North.

In all the operations, marches, and feints, which were so ably performed, and finally resulted in the fall of Columbia, without a battle, the cavalry suffered most. On this important arm of the grand army devolved the strong feint on Augusta, and diversion in favour of the Army of the Tennessee—a similar diversion to that on Forsyth, Macon, and Augusta, in the Georgia campaign. None save those who are well acquainted with the grand strategic movements of Sherman, can fully appreciate the importance of such feints and diversions, and how much rests upon their success.

Thus far, the cavalry with Sherman has never failed. Boldly and skilfully it has operated, despite the superiority in numbers of the enemy's cavalry, and, up to the occupation of Columbia, it had been one continuous skirmish, interspersed with brilliant dashes. The bridge over the Salkehatchie was saved, although on fire, by a daring charge, made by Colonel Van Buskirk and his regiment, the Ninety-second Illinois Mounted Infantry, and Colonel Hamilton's regiment, the Ninth Ohio, which dashed through the swamp and over the burning bridge, routing the enemy from a strong and well-chosen position.

Blackville was taken by a brilliant dash of cavalry, led by Colonel (now Brigadier-General) Jordan and Major Estis. The writer was witness of this spirited affair, and rode in side by side with the brave Colonel Kimel, at the head of the Ninth Pennsylvania, which had the advance. February 7th, six regiments of rebel cavalry, commanded by General Heagan, were totally routed by three small regiments of cavalry, the First Alabama, Fifth Ohio, and Fifth Kentucky, led by Colonel Spencer, in which he captured five battle-flags; and, on the 9th day of the same month, Wheeler's entire force was splendidly repulsed at Johnston's Station.

Wheeler, although a good officer, could not successfully cope with Kilpatrick, and was superseded by Lieutenant-General Wade Hampton, the pet and pride of the chivalry. Against the combined forces of Hampton and Wheeler, Kilpatrick was now forced to contend, and in a few days proved, on the bloodiest cavalry field of the war, his superiority over both.

The same army that had now reached the heart of South Carolina, and occupied her capital city, had, less than one year ago, scaled Stony-faced Ridge, away up among the mountains of Georgia, stormed the rugged hills of Resaca, driven the foe off the far-famed Kenesaw, gazed down upon his retreating columns, had wrested from Georgia her gate-city, and, from Atlanta's burning ruins, had marched in proud triumph to Savannah and the sea! As we look back on those bloody battlefields, rugged mountains, deep ravines, broad rivers, and swamps—hitherto deemed impassable, but over which Sherman led his army to victory, we are lost in wonder and admiration. The flag of the Stars, on the morning of the 17th of February, waved in triumph from the dome of the capitol at Columbia, and in less than three days the city was one vast heap of smouldering ruins.

Sherman was not responsible for this, however; nor did he stop to contemplate the sad spectacle, but pushed boldly forward on his well-studied course. Columbia was now no more. She had "gone glimmering through the dreams of things that were." She resembled ancient Troy, of whom the poet in emphatic language says, "*Troja fuit*"—"*This city has been."* Sherman turned his back on her deserted ruins, and, pursuing his victorious march, soon crossed the State line, and left her, as her capital, now a wilderness. And yet, not a battle had been fought. The Indian defends his *wigwam*, the Mexican his hut, and the Spaniard his towns and cities; but the chivalry of South Carolina, although led by Hampton, Wheeler, Beauregard, and Johnston, had cowardly fled, and that without striking a single blow in defence of their homes and firesides. Well may we hope soon to see the beginning of the end!

While the Army of the Tennessee was resting about Columbia, the left wing and Kilpatrick's cavalry were rapidly pushing forward, crossed the Congaree, and moved to Alston, thirty miles above Columbia. Kilpatrick moved boldly on the extreme left, and, all day marching parallel to and within three miles of the rebel General Cheatham's corps of infantry, reached the railroad, and destroyed the station at Pomona, in advance of him, and then passed down the railroad, destroying the track to the railroad bridge over Broad River. The following day he crossed, moved to Monticello, destroyed the railroad as far up as Shelton's Depot, and then moved across the country towards Chesterfield, covering the infantry until it had successfully crossed the Wateree River; then drew off and marched to Lancaster Court-House, where he found the rebel General Hampton, now in command of all the rebel cavalry.

Fayetteville was Sherman's objective point Kilpatrick was directed to move boldly in towards Charlotte, and so manoeuvre his troops as to convince the enemy that the whole army was moving in that direction. Never was an operation more successfully carried out. Never was an enemy more perfectly deceived. Not only was the enemy deceived, but the deception was kept up for many days, while our army *was hopelessly stuck in the mud*.

The splendid diversion which held Beauregard's army massed to defend Charlotteville, till our army had crossed the Pedee, reflects more credit on Kilpatrick and his command than any previous operation.

While at this point, it was ascertained beyond a doubt that the enemy were killing our soldiers after they had surrendered; but the prompt and determined action of Generals Sherman and Kilpatrick regarding this barbarous warfare initiated by the rebel soldiery, brought it to a sudden termination. An interesting correspondence occurred here on the subject, between Generals Sherman, Kilpatrick, Hampton, and Wheeler. It is given in full, and shows the true temper of these great Union generals, who, upon occasion, handle the pen with the same ease as they wield the sword:

> Headquarters, Cavalry Command,
> Army of Invasion, in the Field, S.C.
> February 22, 1865

Major-General Wheeler,
 Commanding C., S. Cavalry.

General: Yesterday a lieutenant and seven men, and a sergeant of a battery, were taken prisoners by one of your regiments—if I am correctly informed, by a Texas regiment, armed with Spencer carbines, and commanded by a lieutenant-colonel. This officer and his men, after surrendering and being disarmed, were inhumanly and cowardly murdered. Nine of my cavalrymen were also found murdered yesterday—five in a barnyard, three in an open field, and one in the road; two had their throats cut from ear to ear. This makes in all eighteen Federal soldiers murdered yesterday by your people.

Unless some satisfactory explanation be made to me before sundown, February 23rd, I will cause eighteen of your soldiers, now my prisoners, to be shot at that hour; and if this cowardly act be repeated—if my men, when taken, are not treated, in all cases, as prisoners of war should be, I will not only retaliate, as I have already mentioned, but there shall not be left a house standing within reach of my scouting parties along my line of march; nor will I be answerable for the conduct of my soldiers, who will not only be allowed, but encouraged to take a fearful revenge. I know of no other way to intimidate cowards.

I am, General,
> Very respectfully,
> Your obedient Servant,

(Signed)
> J. Kilpatrick,
> Brevet Major-General, Com. Cavalry

> Headquarters, Cavalry Corps
> Chesterfield, S. C.,
> February 22 1865

Major-General Kilpatrick, U.S.A.,
Commanding Cavalry &c.

General: Your dispatch of this date is received, and I am much shocked at the statements which it contains.

I am satisfied you are mistaken in the matter. I have no Texas regiment armed with 'Spencer rifles,' and none commanded by a 'lieutenant-colonel.' The two Texas regiments which belong to my command are commanded by captains, and neither were in any engagement on yesterday. If any of my regiments were engaged with the enemy yesterday, that fact has not yet been reported to me. I will have the matter promptly investigated, and see that full justice is done. Should the report, however, by any means prove correct, I prefer that the retaliation may be inflicted upon the parties guilty of the misdeeds, and not upon innocent persons.

I have no desire, whatever, to make counter-threats in response to those which you have thought proper to address to me; but, should you cause eighteen of my men to be shot, because you *chanced to find that number of your men dead*, I shall regard them as so many murders committed by you, and act accordingly. I trust, however, such a painful necessity will not be forced upon me. Your threat 'to burn every house as far as your scouts can extend,' is of too brutal a character for me, and I think for my government, to attend to.

  Respectfully, Sir,
    Your obedient Servant,
(Signed)   J, Wheeler,
           Major-General C. S. A.

      Headquarters, Cavalry Command,
      Army of Invasion, in the Field, S.C.
         February 23, 1865

Major-General Wheeler,
 Commanding C., S. Cavalry.

"General: Your dispatch, dated Chesterfield, February 22nd, has just been received, and I feel satisfied that you will so fully investigate the circumstances attending the murder of my men, that the guilty parties will be discovered and punished. The regiment referred to as being commanded by a lieutenant-colonel, may have been commanded by a captain; but, certain it is, that the force was mostly composed of Texans, many armed with the Spencer rifle, and my people were shot by order of the officer in command. One of my scouts—a reliable man—was with this force all day, and testified to the fact that not only were these men referred to murdered, bat that the general conversation of your men was, that they would take no more prisoners, I hope you may be able to furnish some reason that may in a degree justify the course taken by your men.

You speak, in your communication, of my threat to burn houses, &c., as being too brutal for you and your government to entertain. No matter how brutal it may seem, I have the power, and will enforce it to the letter; and more, if this course is persisted in, I will not only allow, but encourage my people to retaliate, man for man.

I shall take no action for the present. If stragglers from my command are found in the houses of citizens, committing any outrages whatever, my own people are directed to shoot them upon the spot; and, of course, I expect officers and soldiers of your command to do the same.

I am alive to the fact that I am surrounded by citizens, as well as soldiers, whose bitter hatred to the men I have the honour to command, did not originate with this war, and I expect that some of my men will be killed elsewhere than on the battlefield; but, I know, and shall not hesitate to apply, a severe remedy in each case.

Very respectfully,
Your obedient Servant,
(Signed)   J. Kilpatrick,
Brevet Major-General, Commanding Cavalry.

Headquarters, Division of the Mississippi,
In the Field,
February 24, 1865

Lieutenant-General Wade,
Commanding Cavalry Forces, C.S.A..

General: It is officially reported to me that our foraging parties are murdered after capture, and labelled 'Death to all Foragers.' One instance of a lieutenant and seven men, near Chesterfield, and another of twenty near a ravine, eighty rods from the main road, about three miles from Feasterville. I have ordered a similar number of prisoners in our hands to be disposed of in like manner. I hold about one thousand prisoners, captured in various ways, and can stand it as long as you; but I hardly think these murders are committed by your knowledge, and would suggest that you give notice to the people at large that every life taken by them simply results in the death of one of your confederates.

Of course, you cannot question my right to forage on the country. It is a war-right as old as history. The manner of exercising it varies with circumstances, and if the civil authorities will supply my requisitions, I will forbid all foraging. But I find no civil authorities that can respond to calls for forage or provisions, and therefore must collect directly of the people. I have no doubt this is the occasion of much misbehaviour on the part of our men; but I cannot permit an enemy to judge or punish with wholesale murder.

Personally, I regret the bitter feelings engendered by this war; but they were to be expected, and I simply allege that those who struck the first blow, and made war inevitable, ought not, in fairness, to reproach us for the natural consequences. I merely assert our war-right to forage, and my resolve to protect, to the utmost, my foragers, to the extent of life for life.

    I am, with respect,

           Your obedient Servant,

(Signed)   W. T. Sherman,

                                 Major-General, U. S. A

                           Headquarters, in the Field,

                               February 27, 1865

Major-General W. T. Sherman

United States Army,

General: Your communication of the 24th inst. reached me to-day. In it you state that it has been officially reported that your foraging parties were 'murdered' after capture; and you go on to say that you have ordered a similar number of persons in your hands to be disposed of in like manner; that is to say, you have ordered a number of Confederate soldiers to be 'murdered.'

You characterize your order in proper terms; for the public voice, even in your own country, where it seldom dares to express itself in vindication of truth, honour, or justice, will surely agree with you in pronouncing you guilty of murder, if your order is carried out.

Before discussing this portion of your letter, I beg to assure you for every soldier of mine 'murdered' by you, I shall have executed at once two of yours, giving in all cases preference to any officers who may be in my hands.

In reference to the statement you make regarding the death of your foragers, I have only to say that I know nothing of it, that no orders given by me authorise the killing of prisoners after capture, and that I do not believe my men killed any of yours, except under circumstances in which it was perfectly legitimate and proper they should kill them.

It is a part of the system of the thieves whom you designate as your foragers, to fire the dwellings of those citizens whom they have robbed.

To check this inhuman system, which is fully execrated by every civilized nation, I have directed my men to shoot down all of your men who are caught burning houses. This order shall remain in force as long as you disgrace the profession of arms, by allowing your men to destroy private dwellings.

You say that I cannot, of course, question your right to forage on the country. 'It is a right as old as history.' I do not, sir, question this right. But there is a right, older even than this, and one more inalienable—the right that every man has to defend his home and to protect those who are dependent upon him. And from my heart I wish that every old man and boy in my country, who can fire a gun, would shoot down as he would a wild beast, the men who are desolating their land, burning their houses, and insulting their women.

You are particular in defining and claiming 'war-rights.' May I ask if you enumerate among them the right to fire upon a defenceless city without notice, to burn that city to the ground after it had been surrendered by the authorities, who claimed, though in rain, that protection which is always accorded in civilized warfare to non-combatants; to fire the dwelling-houses of citizens after robbing them, and perpetrate even darker crimes than these—crimes too black to be mentioned?

You have permitted, if you have not ordered, the commission of these outrages against humanity and the rules of war; you fired into the city of Columbia, without a word of warning, after its surrender by the mayor, who demanded protection to private property; you laid the whole city in ashes, leaving amid its ruins thousands of old men and helpless women and children, who are likely to perish of starvation and exposure.

Your line of march can be traced by the lurid light of burning houses, and, in more than one household, there is an agony far more bitter than death. The Indian scalped his victim, regardless of sex or age; but, with all his barbarity, he always respected the persons of his female captives. Your soldiers, more savage than the Indian, insult those whose natural protectors are absent.

In conclusion, I have only to request that when you have any of my men 'disposed of' or 'murdered,' for the terms appear to be synonymous with you, you will let me hear of it, in order that I may know what action to take in the matter. In the meantime, I shall hold fifty-six of your men as hostages for those whom you have ordered to be executed.

I am yours, etc.,

(Signed)   Wade Hampton,
                                      Lieutenant-General

The enemy had been totally deceived, as I before mentioned, and Sherman's various columns were well across Lynch River, and had thrown pontoons across the Pedee, before he could be convinced that Charlotte was *not* to be attacked. Kilpatrick now drew off, crossed Lynch River, moved rapidly for the Pedee, crossed and moved to Rockingham, driving Hampton's cavalry from the town.

Here the cavalry amused Hampton and Hardee until Major-General Slocum had crossed Lynch River; then drew off, and crossing this stream ten miles above, the infantry during the night overcame every obstacle, crossed swamps almost impassable, swollen streams over which the bridges had been destroyed, and after surmounting difficulties that would have disheartened many a commander, hard, dry ground, *terra firma*, was reached at 12 m. on the 9th of March, and Kilpatrick's advance struck Lieutenant-General Hardee's rear guard at Solomon Grove, capturing a number of prisoners. Hardee and Hampton were moving rapidly for Fayetteville. Hampton had not yet arrived, and Kilpatrick determined to intercept this officer and his command, and thus prevent a junction with Hardee at Fayetteville.

I have obtained and give copious extracts from Major-General Kilpatrick's report of the cavalry battle that ensued, and his operations up to the time he reached Fayetteville, N. C.:

Headquarters, Cavalry Command
In the Field,
March 11, 1865

Major Dayton

Major: You will remember that I stated in my last communication, from Solomon's Grove, that Hardee was marching rapidly for Fayetteville, but that Hampton and Wheeler were still in the rear, and that I would endeavour to cut them off. The information was correct. Hampton, however, was found moving upon two roads—the Morgantown road and a road three miles farther to the north, and parallel to it, just south and east of Solomon's Grove.

I posted upon each road a brigade of cavalry, and learning that there was a road still farther north, upon which some of the enemy's troops might move, I made a rapid night's march with Colonel Spencer's little brigade of three regiments, and four hundred dismounted men, and one section of artillery, and took post at the point where the road last mentioned intersects the Morgantown road. During the fore part of the evening, I left General Atkins and joined Colonel Spencer with my staff, and actually rode through one of General Hampton's divisions of cavalry, which, by 11 p. m., had flanked General Atkins, and was then encamped within three miles of Colonel Spencer. My escort of fifteen men and one officer was captured, but I escaped with my staff.

General Atkins and Colonel Jordan discovered, about 9 p.m., that while the enemy was amusing them in front, Hampton was posting with his main force on a road to Atkins's right. These officers at once pulled out, and made every effort to join me before daylight, but failed to do so, owing to bad roads and the almost incessant skirmishing with the enemy, who was marching, and at some points not a mile distant. Hampton had marched all day, and rested his men about three miles from Colonel Jordan's position at 2 a.m., and just before daylight charged my position with three divisions of cavalry, Hume's, Allen's, and Butler's.

Hampton led the centre division, Butler's, and in less than a minute had driven back my men, taken possession of my headquarters, captured my *aide*, and the whole command was flying before the most formidable cavalry charge I ever have witnessed; Colonel Spencer and a large portion of my staff were virtually taken prisoners. On foot, I succeeded in gaining the cavalry command a few hundred yards in the rear, and found the men fighting with the rebels for their camp and animals, and they were soon finally forced back some five hundred yards farther, to a swamp impassable to friend or foe.

The enemy, eager for plunder, failed to promptly follow us up. We rallied, and at once advanced on the foe. We retook the cavalry camp, and, encouraged by our success, charged the enemy who were endeavouring to harness up my battery horses and plundering my headquarters. We retook the artillery, turned it upon the forces about my headquarters, not twenty steps distant, and finally forced him out of my camp with great slaughter.

This is one of the most remarkable instances in which a partial surprise and defeat, by skill and bravery were turned into a most splendid victory. The enemy's loss was most severe. He left upon the field one general officer, two colonels, and over one hundred men killed, and a large number of his wounded. And the houses, for fifteen miles along his line of march, were filled with his wounded. One building alone, in Fayetteville, contained one hundred and three severely wounded. Kilpatrick had, on this occasion, not more than one-third of his command with him, and yet he defeated Hampton's and Wheeler's combined forces.

A portion only of Hampton's troops succeeded in forming a junction with Hardee at Fayetteville, two divisions having been cut off, and forced to move up the Cape Fear River. Kilpatrick now moved to Fayetteville, rested his command a few days, then crossed the river, and moved in the direction of Raleigh, followed by two divisions of the Fourteenth and Twentieth Corps, respectively. He had reached a point about six miles distant from Averysboro, with his advance, encountered a heavy force of rebel infantry, moving down the road from the direction of Raleigh, in line of battle, with skirmishers deployed.

Quick as thought, Kilpatrick dismounted the Ninth Michigan Cavalry, Colonel Acker, and pushed them forward to meet and hold the rebel advance in check, till proper dispositions could be made for the desperate fight which seemed at hand. The roads were almost impassable, the ground low and swampy, and filled with ravines,—a broad, deep ravine, running at right angles with the road, connecting a large swamp on the right with a river on the left. It was evident that the enemy were marching for this ravine, and there intended to defend the road to Raleigh, when they encountered our cavalry.

Kilpatrick was urged by his officers to fell back behind this ravine; that it was dangerous to risk a battle with this ravine in his rear. Said Kilpatrick:

General Sherman must pass this way tomorrow. If the enemy secure this ravine, it will take the whole army to dislodge him. We must look to results, and fight for the success of the campaign; we may get the worst of it, but the enemy must not hold this ravine, if the cavalry can prevent it.

The Ninth Michigan soon became hotly engaged with the enemy, and, by splendid fighting, held him in check until Kilpatrick had taken up a strong position, dismounted, with his flanks resting upon the ravine, and his front fortified with rails, brush, and timber. Meantime, *aide* after *aide* had been dispatched to General Sherman, six miles in the rear, for infantry re-enforcements. The enemy, having deployed his lines, finally advanced, driving the Ninth Michigan Cavalry back into the woods.

But now the rapid and destructive fire from Captain Beebe's artillery soon forced him to halt, and, finally, to fall back under cover of a ravine a thousand yards distant. It was now dark, and our troops rested upon their arms. During the night, a brigade of infantry came up, and with his cavalry and this force General Kilpatrick moved forward in line of battle at daylight, the infantry having the centre, a strong force of cavalry, under Colonels Jones and Spencer, moving upon either flank, while the artillery and the majority of the cavalry, under General Atkins, held the rear. Kilpatrick had not moved a mile from out his works, when the pickets of the enemy were encountered and driven in, and in a few minutes his whole skirmish line became engaged, telling him that he had met the enemy in force. He extended his lines upon the right and left, and soon forced the enemy in upon his line of battle, and drawing the fire of his artillery.

The enemy, believing that cavalry alone was making the attack, took the offensive, moved from right to left, and rapidly bore down upon the cavalry under Colonel Jones, who held the right. This movement was discovered in sufficient time to re-enforce the right, and Colonel Jordan, with his cavalry brigade, reached the point threatened before the attack was made, and, with Colonel Jones and his command, dismounted, handsomely repulsed three determined charges, and finally forced the enemy back, and into his line of works.

In the meantime, Kilpatrick had thoroughly reconnoitred the entire position, and had sent for and received a second brigade of infantry, which was pushed in upon our left, with instructions to carry the enemy's works upon his right. While this was being done, the enemy again moved out of his works, and furiously attacked the cavalry on the right. General Atkins was now brought up, and pushed in to the assistance of Colonel Jordan. At this moment, the shout of the infantry, upon the left, as they rushed forward to storm the enemy's works, was heard. A general advance was at once ordered, and the enemy was driven back at all points, over and out of his first line of works, with the loss of three pieces of artillery and many prisoners. The Twentieth Corps, under General Williams, had in the meantime come up, as well as a portion of the Fourteenth, General Davis, and under the personal direction of Major-General Slocum, commanding the left wing, was sent forward into position, and steadily pressed the enemy back, until late in the night, when, under cover of the darkness, he retreated in the direction of Raleigh.

In this engagement (16th of March) the cavalry fought, side by side with our infantry, mounted and dismounted, and behaved most gallantly. Charge after charge of the enemy's infantry was repulsed; and Colonel Jones, of the Eighth Indiana Cavalry, actually rode over the enemy's works, losing one-third of his entire command. Our cavalry, cm this day, won the admiration of the entire army.

During the night, Kilpatrick withdrew his command, crossed Black River, and moved off, upon the Smithfield road, to the left and front of the main army, now moving on Goldsboro. The following day, Lieutenant-General Johnston evacuated Goldsboro, and massed his forces at the little town of Bentonsville, on Mill Creek, midway between Raleigh and Goldsboro, and there, behind strong intrenchments, resolved to dispute the further advance of Sherman's victorious columns.

This was the last battle of the campaign in which the cavalry command took an active part, though it remained on the field ready to take part in the tattle of Bentonsville, which took place on the 19th.

Such an opportunity, however, did not present itself; for the enemy, defeated and driven beyond Mill Creek, the main body of the army moved to Goldsboro, and the cavalry command to Mount Olive, on the Wilmington military railroad, and there went into camp.

Here it rested after its labours, sufferings, and dangers, in the glorious campaign through which it had passed.

It had stood out in bold relief before a whole army, and, had it never gained a laurel before that day, its deeds of daring and success would have been rendered immortal for the unflinching, heroic, and most gallant services rendered during this glorious campaign, now brought to a close. The arms of the command, in all its hard struggles, had ever been crowned with success; and the reverses chronicled by most narrators of military events, ancient and modem, it has never been our misfortune to have to record. It is our pleasure and pride, on the contrary, to lay before the people the congratulations of the general-in-chief, one who ranks with renowned conquerors, celebrated in song and story:

Military Division of the Mississippi
In the Field,
March 22, 1865

Special Field Orders

No. 35

The general commanding announces to this army, that it beat, on its chosen ground, the concentrated armies of our enemy, who has fled in disorder, leaving his dead, wounded, and prisoners in our hands, and burning his bridges on his retreat.

On the same day, Major-General Schofield, from Newbern, entered and occupied Goldsboro, and Major-General Terry, from Wilmington, secured Cox's Bridge crossing, and laid a pontoon bridge, so that our campaign has resulted in a glorious success, after a march of the most extraordinary character, near five hundred miles, over swamps and rivers deemed impassable to others, at the most inclement season of the year, and drawing our chief supplies from a poor and wasted country.

I thank the army, and assure it that our government and people honour them for this new display of physical and moral qualities, which reflect honour upon the whole nation.

You shall now have rest, and all the supplies that can be brought from the rich granaries and storehouses of our magnificent country, before again embarking on new and untried dangers.

W. T. Sherman,
Major-General Commanding:
Brevet Major-General J. Kilpatrick.

The wounded and sick, in this famous campaign, were attended with all the surgical and medical skill necessary; and it may be truly said that the Medical Director, Dr. Helm, and all the medical officers, promptly, and in the face of dangers, responded to every call of duty, But, in a long and wearisome march, ambulances broke down, or stuck in the mud, and often had to be abandoned. Of all the officers in this campaign, the medical officers were not the least painfully taxed; and the skill, humanity, and promptness with which their duties were executed, are worthy the highest praise.

It was after the battle above described, and while resting on the laurels he and his men so dearly won, that the appreciation of Sherman, and the words of praise he spoke, made the heart of the cavalry leader to thrill, and filled it with the true exultation known to generous minds, and Kilpatrick issued the following congratulatory address to his brave men:

> Headquarters, Cavalry Command
> In the Field,
> March 22, 1865

(Circular)

The campaign is over, and we are promised rest. Our depot will be at Mount Olive, and a railroad shall be at the disposal of officers and men. Every liberty shall be granted consistent with the best interests of our cause, for which I feel in my heart the invincible soldiers of my command have done so much. This day I met our great chief on the field of battle, amid the dead and dying of our enemy, who has again fled before our proud advancing banners, and my ears were made to tingle with the grateful words of praise, spoken in admiration of the cavalry.

Soldiers, be proud! Of all the brave men of this great army, you have a right to be. You have won the admiration of our infantry, fighting on foot, and mounted, and you will receive the outspoken words of praise from the great Sherman himself.

He appreciates and will reward your patient endurance of hardships, gallant deeds, and valuable services.

With the old laurels of Georgia, entwine those won in the Carolinas, and proudly wear them!

General Sherman is satisfied with his Cavalry,

By command of Brevet Major-General Kilpatrick.

(Signed)   S. G. Estis,
                                                                              Major and A. A. G.

These men, in toil, clanger, and battle, did their duty. To have been of, and with them, is the writer's pride. A grateful nation will never forget them. Their ranks are thinned; many rest in the quiet of the grave. But the services rendered the nation are worthy of imitation by all posterity; and, long as the Republic lasts, their memorials will continue to exist. How freely they offered their lives a sacrifice at the altar of their country! How gladly, on the most sanguinary fields of the rebellion, they met the enemy, will be told in terms of eulogy by historians and poets in future generations.

Conclusion

In this comparatively brief space have been related the events which, in connection with a portion of the cavalry, took place in dangerous and fatiguing marches, in uncomfortable bivouac, in the skirmish and the battle-lines, and in bloodshed, death, and victory. What a picture does such a narrative form! How incongruous are all the elements that enter into the composition, and yet how they harmonize in grand achievement! A plain narration of facts, without colouring or exaggeration, has been our aim. To tell the reader what was done, and the way it was done, was the purpose in view; and, in the execution of the design, there has been no conscious deviation.

It is by no means assumed that, in this sketch, full justice has been done the subject, though, perhaps, more battles and events of importance are herein narrated than will be found in some more pretentious volumes; that many of these events in full detail would require a volume, and yet another to include the innumerable incidents illustrating the personal courage, daring, and patriotism displayed upon every field, we are well aware; but such an account in the present work was out of the question, as moderate space was imperatively demanded. Had not this been the case, it would have been a profit as well as pleasure to linger also amid the romantic scenery of the Cumberland Mountains, and the classic ground from Murfreesboro to Atlanta, through the centre of Georgia, and in the varied country of the Carolinas.

Vividly could be described the bold outlines of the mountain-mass, the rocks which in colossal grandeur have stood immovable for ages, bearing in their bosom the records of a past, in which the geologist traces an interesting history of the animal and vegetable kingdoms, in comparison to which centuries are as days; the steep ascent of Lookout Mountain, or of Mission Ridge, and the gloomy brow of

Kenesaw, which looked down on as grand and heroic efforts as the world ever witnessed. When Titus beheld the strong fortifications of Jerusalem, he exclaimed that to take them was impossible, had not Divine aid enabled him to do so. Must not the same be said of the endless earthworks that, around Atlanta, indicate the fierce struggle of armies, and the mighty force arrayed required to hurl rebellion from its defences?

In describing such scenes, it is necessary to trace the line of the Chickamauga, and, with the wand of an enchanter, conjure up again the armies that there contended; and, listening to the discordant bat-tle-sounds, the roar of artillery, and the clash of arms, would be like witnessing the mighty efforts for the ascendency.

The graves of our fallen patriots might have claimed a tributary tear! The little headboards that mark the last resting-place of so many poor fellows, dear in life, could be transmuted into a living volume, in which a life history would be recorded—its hopes, fears, joys, and sor-rows—of those departed heroes, every incident of whose career must ever be of interest to all, but more especially to us, their comrades.

We might have pointed out the opulent plantation, in the march through Georgia and the Carolinas, on which peace and plenty smiled, and where lived a once happy household, with every comfort in life. The story is soon told. Rebellion and its results: the men go to the war; the slaves run away; the cotton is destroyed—fired by a torch; foragers remove the supplies, and the family, once so prosperous and happy, is without a meal.

The tale of our progress, in the march of Sherman's victorious army, will be illustrated by the future historian and novelist, who will, with more vividness and imagery, depict the scenes, and in thrilling narratives describe the story of the war, in words of never-ending interest, with incidents of heroism, and love of country, furnishing worthy subjects of imitation to the youth of the greatest Republic that ever existed: and the results of the rebellion will stand a warning to future generations, to avoid the insubordination and unfaithfulness ending in disaster and ruin. No war has been more fruitful in events interesting in their character and important to the world in example.

The reader has, in *Kilpatrick and our Cavalry*, a condensed account of the events in the life of that general, which, from an early day to the point of time where this volume closes, from a life thus far as active and eventful, in the main, as seldom falls to the lot of a young man of the age of seven-and-twenty. When it was urged upon the writer to give some account of the operations of our cavalry under his command, he little considered how laborious and difficult an undertaking it was. A few data, reference to reports and documents, and eyes and ears, were considered sufficient. But apart from the difficulties of composition in the field, and the active professional duties of a medical officer in a campaign, where his services were in constant requisition, it proved no easy task. To say nothing of the difficulties in other respects, there remained the important one of ascertaining facts, where he was not an eye-witness, and of which there were no records.

In passing through the Carolinas, and crossing those swamps and rivers, classical and historical, the scenes in which Marion was an actor were often brought to mind. The name of this active cavalry leader will forever live in the minds of the people. He was the fox of the swamps, whose vigilance, ever prepared for the foe, often brought down punishment on his head; and when pursued by a superior force, his men disbanded, and could not be found. The services rendered his country were important, and our cavaliers were animated by remembrance of so bright an example. The reader may consult the map, on which can be traced the scenes in which our forces followed in the footsteps of Sumter and Marion, of Gates or of Greene, in the struggle for freedom, amid the swamps and rivers of South Carolina,

The day is not distant when the vast territory of the States traversed by our cavalry, shall undergo, an important change in the reconstruction of ruined homesteads and broken-down estates: a more perfect system of agriculture; the supply of free labour, and the improvement by energy, industry, and capital, of the resources of a country capable of much amelioration, and unbounded development in the arts, commerce, and navigation.

It will be then, when population spreads, when churches, schools, and colleges multiply, when a free press throughout the South shall minister to a people free from the shackles of a hateful oligarchy, and unbiassed by demagogues, shall, under the old banner of the Republic, rejoice and sing, and sweet music resound in all the borders of this sunny land.

And when the last cavalryman is no more when the leader himself has gone, their glorious deeds of old will be brought to mind; and so shall it be, as the stream of Time flows on to the eternal sea, and the people, devoted to agriculture and peaceful pursuits, shall turn over with the ploughshare some old shell, sabre, or carbine, relics of the battlefield, then shall be remembered by some hoary sage the tradition of his youth regarding it, and, with his aged and quaking arm, and the staff that sustains his tottering frame, he shall point out the former battle-line, and describe how the men rallied to their leader, as Kilpatrick led them on to battle and to victory.

Honour the brave and bold!
Long shall the tale be told.
Yea, when our babes are old,
How they rode onward!

Yours truly
Joseph G. Vale

The Kilpatrick Raid
By Joseph G. Vale

Hurrah! the foes are moving. Hark to the mingled din
Of fife and steed, and trump and drum, and roaring culverin.
The fiery duke is pricking fast across Saint Andre's plain,
With all the hireling chivalry of Guelders and Almayne.
Now by the lips of those ye love, fair gentlemen of France,
Charge for the golden lilies now, upon them with the lance!
A thousand spurs are striking deep, a thousand spears at rest,
A thousand knights are pressing close behind the snow-white crest;
And in they burst and on they rushed, while, like a guiding star,
Amid the thickest carnage, blazed the helmet of Navarre.
—Macauley—The Battle of Ivey.

At 10 o'clock on the morning of August 18th, Minty, commanding the First and Second brigades, marched from camp near Peach Tree creek, north-east of Atlanta, with the following forces: First brigade. Colonel R. H. G. Minty, commanding: Fourth United States cavalry, eleven officers, two hundred and sixty-two men, Captain McIntyre; Seventh Pennsylvania cavalry, sixteen officers, three hundred and thirteen men. Major W. W, Jennings; Fourth Michigan, nineteen officers, two hundred and thirty-one men, Major Frank Mix; headquarters, eight officers, sixty-five men; total, fifty-four officers, nine hundred and twenty-five men; aggregate, nine hundred and twenty-five.

Second brigade, Colonel Eli Long, commanding: First Ohio Cavalry, sixteen officers, three hundred and thirty men, Colonel Eggleston; Third Ohio, twenty-seven officers, four hundred and fifty men. Colonel Murray; Fourth Ohio, twenty -four officers, four hundred and fifty-five men; head-quarters, eight officers, seventy-three men; total, seventy-five officers, thirteen hundred and three men; aggregate, thirteen hundred and eighty-three. Chicago Board of Trade battery, two officers, eighty-eight men; four guns; aggregating ninety officers and men, making a total aggregate of two thousand three hundred and ninety-eight officers and men, and four guns.

At 6 a.m., on reaching the banks of Utoy Creek, he halted for a short time, then, resuming the march, reached Sandtown, where, in obedience to orders of General Gerrard, he reported to Major General Kilpatrick, commanding the Third cavalry division. By orders of General Kilpatrick, he marched at dusk of that evening, in rear of the Third division, reaching at daybreak of the 19th, the Montgomery and Atlanta railroad, at Red bank, west of Atlanta. While the First brigade was crossing the railroad, a battery of rebel artillery posted on the hills east and parallel to the line of march, and supported by a brigade of mounted infantry, suddenly assailed with great fury on the left flank. The rebels, under cover of the mist, pushed up to within two hundred yards of the marching column, opening with artillery and musketry on the Seventh Pennsylvania, then passing.

The head of the regiment having already reached the Atlanta and Jonesboro' dirt road, passed on, following the Fourth United States, the advance regiment of the brigade. Companies G and M, although exposed to the full force of, and consequent confusion resulting from, the unexpected attack, were held firmly in place, and, closing ranks, pushed through the heavy fire, and finding a rebel force barring their way at the junction of the Sandtown with the Jonesboro' road, charged and scattered, and drove them several hundred yards in the direction of Atlanta; and then closed up on the leading companies. Major Davis, however, commanding the rear battalion of the regiment, not knowing what the condition of affairs in the front might be, after a slight skirmish, formed line eastward of the road; and, on the arrival of Major Mix, with the Fourth Michigan, reported the situation to him.

Immediately in the rear of the Fourth Michigan were the ambulances and pack-mules of the brigade; Mix, therefore, promptly deployed his regiment, after slightly advancing the left of Davis, on the left of this battalion, the line thus facing south-east, and moving the whole force forward attacked the rebels with great vigour, and in about half an hour drove them in confusion from the position, and re-united the column; then, wheeling eastward, pursued them rapidly for over a mile and a half. On learning of the attack, Minty halted the First brigade and sent the Fourth United States to continue the pursuit, which it did three miles, and, returning, reported that the whole rebel force was in full and confused retreat.

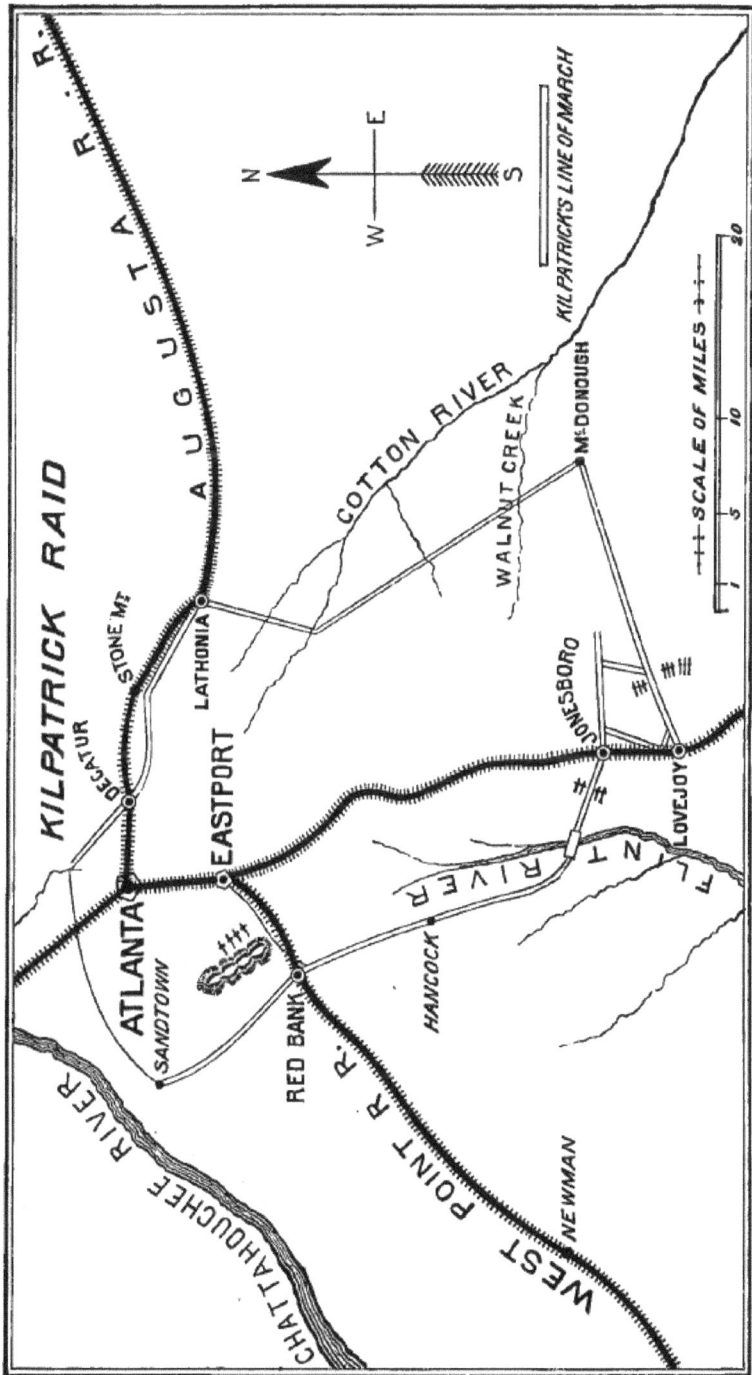

KILPATRICK RAID

KILPATRICK'S LINE OF MARCH

SCALE OF MILES

N E S W

AUGUSTA R. R.

STONE M.T
DECATUR
LATHONIA
COTTON RIVER
WALNUT CREEK
McDONOUGH
JONESBORO
LOVEJOY
FLINT RIVER
HANCOCK
EASTPORT
ATLANTA
SANDTOWN
RED BANK
WEST POINT R. R.
NEWMAN
CHATTAHOUCHEE RIVER

While Majors Mix and Davis were attacking the rebel force, one of the ambulance drivers, Wilson H. Smith, (known as "Limerick,") finding the shells bursting over and around him, attempted to run the fire and join the column; two other ambulances followed this one, drawing upon themselves the fire of several of the guns. "Limerick" took to the woods on the right of the road, and, putting his mules to the run, forced his way through, but with a very badly used up ambulance. In fact, he brought out with him very little more than the mules, harness, the running-gear, and the badly smashed body of the vehicle; the bows, cover, seats, cushions, &c., being left behind. The second ambulance kept the road, and got through with numerous bullet holes and slightly shattered by a shell. The other one was wrecked in the woods. Oran F. Wilson, of company G., was killed at the junction of the roads, as Captains Garrett and Vale charged through.

On resuming the march, Minty was directed to take the advance, the enemy having appeared in force in front. He soon discovered that the only rebel force was Ross' brigade of cavalry, and finding the woods so thick that better progress could be made on foot, dismounted the Second brigade and advanced as rapidly as the men could walk, driving the rebels steadily before him until the banks of the Flint river were reached. It was here found that the enemy, reinforced by Ferguson's brigade, had destroyed the bridge, and taken a fortified position on the other side, from which they opened on us with artillery.

Lieutenant Bennett, with the Chicago Board of Trade battery, immediately opened on their battery, and soon silenced it; upon which, General Kilpatrick ordered up the remaining guns, under Lieutenant Robinson, and, placing the whole eight pieces in position, directed the rebel lines should be shelled by volleys. At the fourth discharge, Minty advanced his whole division, dismounted, to a slightly sheltered position, along the bank of the river, and opening a deadly fire from his carbines, soon drove the enemy from their works. The Second brigade, with the Fourth United States and Fourth Michigan, crossed the river on the stringers of the ruined bridge, and, promptly deploying, continued the advance. The bridge was rapidly repaired, when the whole command crossed, and, with the dismounted men as skirmishers, drove Ross and Ferguson into the town of Jonesboro', where they, taking shelter in the buildings, continued the fight, until Minty, getting his artillery in position, formed storming columns and ordered an advance at a double quick. Upon this advance, under cover of the guns, the rebels mounted and retreated in confusion, and the town and railroad were won.

Thus, Minty and his cavalry were the first of the Union Army to stand on the only remaining link of supplies and communication uniting Hood's army and Atlanta with the Confederacy. But merely taking possession was not enough—the road must be destroyed, and that so thoroughly as to prevent its use for some time, for Sherman to reap any advantage from our movement. The work of destruction was quickly begun, and perseveringly prosecuted, under a continuous, heavy fire from the rebels, now reinforced by a brigade of infantry, brought down from Atlanta. Leaving the Third division to complete the work, Minty was ordered to post his First brigade across the railroad, facing toward Atlanta, and repel the enemy.

A sharp fight ensued, but though he had three brigades against his one, he held the enemy in check for over two hours, when, bringing up the Second brigade, he maintained his position until, at 10. p. m., he was ordered to fall back down the road, covering the Third division, with which the general proposed to move south, and continue the work of destroying the road. Up to this time, six miles of track, and all the railroad buildings, with two thirds of the town, had been destroyed.

On reaching the designated position. Colonel Murray, of the Fourth Ohio, was ordered to advance, but finding the enemy, by this time, in heavy force, and strongly posted behind barricades and breastworks, failed to dislodge them, and fell back to the main line. The object of the whole movement being only the destruction of the railroad, Kilpatrick, not wishing to get his men entangled in any controversy with the enemy which would delay or interfere with that object, now determined on a flank movement: first, toward McDonough, then westward, until he again should strike the road, continuing this operation down the road until it was completely destroyed. He, therefore, directed Minty to take the advance with his own brigade, and move out on the McDonough road, while Colonel Long, with his brigade, formed the rear of the column, Minty to remain with the Second brigade.

The column moved about 4 a.m., toward McDonough, for about five miles, when it was halted to feed—the horses corn; the men, coffee and crackers—at a place where a road leading southward intersected the one east to McDonough. While here halted, the rear brigade, commanded by Colonel Long, was attacked by the rebel column, which had followed from Jonesboro'. Colonel Long promptly deployed his magnificent command of Ohio boys, and waiting until the enemy—two brigades of cavalry fighting on foot and one of infantry—had advanced within effective striking distance, pushed his men out in a counter-charge and in half an hour repulsed the whole rebel force, driving them back, in confusion, on Jonesboro'. While this fight was in progress, the column resumed its march. General Kilpatrick remarking that "Long can easily attend to them fellows," turning sharply to the right, or southward. In making this turn, the larger part of the column had a capital opportunity of enjoying a fight— that is, of seeing Long's without being in it.

The road we were on led directly, though with numerous turns around and among the hills, to Lovejoy station, which, like Jonesboro', is on the Macon railroad. About a mile and a half from the station, the road forks, or, rather, a branch road, leading slightly north, runs to the railroad, about a mile from the station, while the direct road, about half a mile further on, also turns somewhat northward, and leads direct to Lovejoy. After the repulse of the rebels in our rear—that portion now being considered safe from attack—Long's brigade was brought to the front and joined the First, falling in behind it, at the head of the column, Kilpatrick seeming to be desirous of complimenting the Second division by giving it the precedence whenever a fight was imminent, no matter whether in front or rear! At this time, about 9 a. m., it began to be noticed that mounted rebel videttes were watching and reporting the progress and direction of the column, always, however, keeping at such a safe distance as rendered pursuit useless.

Minty detached the Fourth Michigan cavalry, under Major Mix, on the right-hand road, with orders to gain possession of and destroy the railroad north of the station. The particular object of this movement, in addition to damaging the road as much as possible, was to prevent the anticipated return of a train, which the general thought he had heard pass up the road toward Jonesboro', but which, in fact, had only gone as far as Lovejoy. The main column moved on the direct road toward the station, and when within about a mile of it the advance guard—a battalion of the Seventh Pennsylvania, under Major Dartt—became heavily engaged.

The woods on the roadside were very thick. and it being desirable to get on the railroad as soon as possible, the head of the column was pushed more rapidly than the dismounted skirmishers could clear the flanks, so that when about half a mile from the station the mounted column had several hundred yards of flank exposed and unprotected.

The direction which the road ran led this portion of the command, for about two hundred yards, along the front of a full brigade of rebel infantry, lying in a depression, or, probably, a cut of the railroad. The order to "trot" had been given, when a volley from the concealed foe crashed through the ranks.

The men of the Seventh dismounted immediately and formed in line, when Colonel Minty, coming up at the head of the Fourth United States, received a like volley, gave the command, "Prepare to fight on foot," and formed the Fourth United States on the right of the Seventh Pennsylvania. The two regiments moved forward at once, and drove the enemy back to the railroad, where another brigade of infantry rose from the embankment, delivered an oblique fire, raking the line from left to right; then, fixing bayonets, rushed forward in a charge against our left, while the force in front, re-forming, joined in the bayonet charge. The men of the two regiments stood firmly until they had emptied the seven loads contained in their carbine magazines, when, not having time to refill them, were forced back in utter defeat and badly cut to pieces. Six hundred dismounted cavalry pitted against nearly three thousand of the best soldiers of Pat Clayburn's famous division was more than they could stand.

The four guns of Minty's command, now taking position in a cornfield, slightly to the left, checked the rebel onslaught by the gastric use of canister from three of the pieces, while the fourth exploded shells in their midst.

At the time the head of the column was thus being repulsed and cut to pieces near the station, the rear was attacked, about a mile and a half off, by Martin's and Ross' divisions of cavalry, and two brigades of Clayburn's division of infantry, with eight pieces of artillery. The rear regiments were driven in about a mile, or almost to the point where the road forks. The Third division, with four pieces of its artillery, was immediately formed in line at the forks of the road, facing southward, to check this attack, while Long's brigade formed, with the remainder of the First, in the field supporting its battery. Heavy and continuous firing was maintained in both the front and rear portions of the command, the rebel volleys and cheers in our front being echoed by rebel volleys and cheers in our rear!

The enemy's line now advanced from the station to the edge of the woods, on three sides of Lieutenant Robinson's Chicago Board of Trade battery, and opening a galling fire on it from front and both flanks, forced it to fall back to the same hill occupied by the guns of the Third division, leaving one of the pieces, which had been disabled, on the field, after losing twelve *per cent*, of the men and two thirds of the horses. The abandoned gun was, however, immediately after brought in by volunteers from the Fourth Michigan Cavalry, taken off the broken carriage, and placed in a wagon. Meanwhile, Colonel Long's brigade, though hard pressed, succeeded in holding the force from the station in check, and prevented its advance beyond the edge of the woods.

General Kilpatrick now directed the whole force to mount, and form facing the rear, preparatory to a charge. Two well-equipped and powerful cavalry expeditions had been sent previous to owes, to cut this same Atlanta and Macon road; the first, under General McCook, after destroying the West Point road, had, on approaching the Ma-con, been defeated and driven in disordered fragments into our lines; while the second, under Stoneman, after slightly damaging the road near Macon, was repulsed in an attack on that city, and being widely scattered over the country, was almost entirely captured, Stoneman himself surrendering the larger portion, which, remaining with him, had maintained its organization. Kilpatrick was now confronted with a far greater force than had been employed by the rebels in the defeat of either McCook or Stoneman; he, however, was a cavalry general, and avoiding the fatal errors of his predecessors, in scattering his com-mand, was able to bring his united force to bear in this emergency.

The rebels, on finding the railroad cut at Jonesboro' had dispatched Clayburn's division, four brigades of infantry and twelve pieces of artillery, from Atlanta, and sending. Martin's division of cavalry to rein-force Ross and Ferguson, had assembled this united force at Jonesboro' on the morning of the 20th, about daybreak. A brigade of infantry, with six pieces of artillery, had also been sent up the road from Macon, and was halted at Lovejoy station. A force, known as the Independent brigade, of about one thousand State troops, also moved from a point south of Lovejoy, and, approaching the station, formed in on the left of the rebel force in our rear. Shortly after daylight, two brigades of Clay-burn's men moved down the railroad, while Ross and Ferguson, with two brigades of Clayburn's infantry, marched in pursuit, following the rear of our column. Martin, with his division, joined this pursuing force at the point where we had halted for breakfast.

It thus appears that the rebels had on the ground, now surround-ing Kilpatrick, five brigades of infantry, eighteen pieces of artillery, and six brigades of cavalry, in all a force of twelve thousand men of al arms. Kilpatrick had, as before stated, the Second division, numbering two thousand three hundred and ninety-eight men and four pieces of artillery, one of which was disabled and useless, and the Third division, numbering two thousand four hundred men and four pieces of artillery, in all four thousand seven hundred and ninety-eight cavalry and seven guns.

After forming, his command faced to the rear, Kilpatrick directed Minty to lead the charge with his, the Second, division. Minty formed, placing the First brigade in the advance; on the right or west side; of the road, in regimental columns of fours, the Seventh Pennsylvania, under Major Jennings, on the right, the Fourth United States, under Captain McIntyre, on the left, and the Fourth Michigan, under Major Mix, in the centre; the distance between the columns being about one hundred and fifty yards. Two companies, B and M, of the Seventh Pennsylvania were deployed in front as skirmishers, and directed, covering the whole front, to throw down the first of the intervening fences.

As soon as the skirmishers reached the fence, the advance was sounded, followed, after passing the fence, by the "gallop" and the "charge," and Minty hurled his three columns, in a terrific burst of flashing steel, upon three points of the rebel lines. In anticipation of something of the kind being attempted, the rebel infantry had been formed in three lines, about fifty yards apart, in double rank; the first and second lines with fixed bayonets and the third line firing; in both the first and second lines the front rank knelt on one knee, resting the butt of the gun on the ground, the bayonet at a "charge."

Immediately on the charging columns showing themselves, the enemy opened with shell from four pieces of artillery in our front, and from six pieces on our right front, canister was, after the first or second discharge, substituted for shell, by the battery in our front. After the columns had passed the first fence, the infantry and cavalry opened a fire of musketry. Through this storm of shell, canister, and musketry, the charging columns, closely followed by the gallant Long and his brigade of intrepid Ohioans, in column of regiments, swept over the fields, broken though the ground was with deep gulleys or washouts, leaping over three sets of out-lying rail barricades, and, without firing a shot, reached the rebel first line, posted slightly in the rear of a fence.

The rebel cavalry broke and fled in the wildest panic, just before we struck them, but the infantry stood firm. Leaping, in maddened rush at the top of speed, our horses over the fence, and where this could not be done, dashing with impetuous force against it, the impediment was passed, without drawing rein, and, with their keen blades, the brigade in an instant cut the rebel front line to pieces! rode over, and destroyed it! and assailed with renewed vigour their second line. Between the first and second lines, the columns obliqued slightly to the left, and, striking it thus on a half left turn, presented somewhat the appearance of a movement by platoons in "*echelon*," assaulting it in many places in quick succession, penetrated and sabreed it to pieces as quickly as they had the first! The third line now broke and ran in utter confusion and rout, but we were soon among them, riding down and sabreing hundreds as they ran.

The formation of the brigade led the Seventh Pennsylvania squarely against the left centre of the infantry, the Fourth Michigan against its right, and the rebel battery, and the Fourth United States against the battery, and that part of the rebel line held by their cavalry. After cutting the enemy's lines to pieces, the Seventh Pennsylvania and Fourth Michigan, making a full left wheel, dashed upon the artillery, sabreing the gunners beside their pieces the while. Three of the pieces, all we had horses for, were brought off, and the other one was disabled by spiking, blowing up the caissons and chopping to pieces the wheels.

The race and slaughter among the fleeing rebels was then continued for three miles, when Minty halted and re-formed his command, now badly scattered. It was understood that the Second brigade of ours, and the Third division, should follow the charge of Minty's brigade in line, thus securing the full fruits of the conflict, but by some mistake. Colonel Long formed in column of companies, or battalions, and joined in the charge, following rapidly through the rebel lines, while the Third division, holding the column of fours, followed the road; hence the masses of the enemy, which had been run over by the First brigade, were not gathered up, nor was any effort made to ascertain the number of killed and wounded.

Minty's task being simply to crush and destroy the rebel lines, he made no effort to take prisoners, only requiring the enemy to destroy their guns as he passed through. This much is, however, known: over four thousand of the rebel infantry were either killed, wounded, or at one time disarmed prisoners in our hands. The change of formation made in the Third division left this most brilliant affair almost barren of results, even the four hundred prisoners taken by the brigade in the last pursuit, after having been turned over to the other command, were allowed to escape.

Colonel Long was, however, fully justified in supporting the advance brigade of his division by the full force of his splendid brigade, for the charge of the First brigade looked to be such a desperate undertaking that its success was deemed almost impossible, but there was certainly no reason why the Third division should not have swept forward in line and brought off our own wounded and the entire disarmed host of the enemy. Minty, however, brought inside our lines three pieces of artillery and three stands of colours, to wit: The Third Texas cavalry, Zachariah Rangers, and Benjamin's infantry, and turned over to the Third division more than four hundred prisoners, which he captured in the pursuit after breaking through the lines.

After re-forming his command, Minty was directed by General Kilpatrick to cover the march of the column toward McDonough. The Second brigade, under Colonel Long, was, therefore, formed in line of battle, facing westward. It took some time for the column to pass, and before it got fairly on its way. Long was furiously assailed by the rebel force advancing from Lovejoy station, consisting of the forces before noted as gathered there. Colonel Long, with his gallant Second brigade of Ohio regiments, was here engaged in a most desperate battle for over two hours; but, although largely outnumbered, himself desperately wounded, and his command reduced over ten *per cent*, in killed and wounded, he defeated the enemy entirely, and successfully "covered the column."

After Colonel Long was wounded, the command of his brigade devolved upon Colonel Egglanton, of the First Ohio, who commanded the latter part of the battle, with skill and success. The Third division being now well on its march, Minty directed Colonel Egglanton to break into column and follow, placing the Seventh Pennsylvania, the Fourth Michigan, and Lieutenant Bennett's section of artillery in position in line to cover the movement. General Clayburn, now in command of the rebel forces, rallied his men, and advanced under cover of the rapid fire of six pieces of artillery. The two regiments hastily constructed barricades of fence rails, and successfully beat them back without suffering heavy loss, for while the artillery fire was rapid and noisy, the enemy did not seem inclined to press the issue to close quarters.

As the rear of the Second brigade passed this position, one of Bennett's guns burst, and soon after the other was rendered useless by the wedging in of a shell. The rapid firing of the "seven shooters" of the Fourth and Seventh held the enemy in check, however, until the road was clear, when the command was mounted, and following in the rear of the others, marched in the direction of McDonough.

A heavy rain began soon after, and continued in tremendous showers all night, through which and the deep, splashing mud we marched, passing through McDonough about midnight, and halting in short bivouac about 2 a.m., on the 21st, on the north bank of Walnut Creek. During this night's march, the column was considerably scattered, and the prisoners captured in the great charge generally escaped. The halt at Walnut creek was so short that the rear of the column scarcely noticed it, for about the time the column closed up the march was resumed. About 6, a.m., we reached the south bank of the Cotton River, which, now swollen to an enormous height, had swept away the bridge.

In the course of a couple of hours, the waters subsided sufficiently to enable the command to cross by swimming the horses over a swift, though narrow, channel. In this crossing, the First brigade lost one man and fifty horses, and nearly all the pack-mules drowned. All the cooking and mess-kits of the companies were lost. It being impossible to get the wagon with the two disabled guns in across, the guns were taken out and buried, the site marked as the graves of two soldiers of the Fourth United States cavalry, and the wagon burned. After a long, continuous march, we reached Lithonia, on the Augusta railroad, and went into bivouac about 9, p.m., and next day, 22nd, marching through Latimer and Decatur, reached our camp at Peach Tree creek, having made a complete circuit of both armies in five days. Minty says, in his official report:

> Every officer and man in the command acted so well, so nobly, so gallantly, that under ordinary circumstances they would be entitled to special mention. Day and night, from the 18th to the 22nd, these gallant men were without sleep, and almost without food. During that time, they marched and skirmished almost incessantly; fought four pitched battles, and swam a flooded river, without once complaining or murmuring!
>
> I cannot close this necessarily long report without calling attention to the magnificent manner in which the Chicago Board of Trade battery was fought by Lieutenants Robinson and Bennett on every occasion on which it was brought into action.
>
> Colonel Long, Second brigade, and the regimental commanders, distinguished themselves by the able manner in which they

handled their commands."

Captain McIntyre, Fourth United States cavalry, rendered himself conspicuous by the gallant manner in which he led his command on the 20th.

Private Samuel Walters, Seventh Pennsylvania cavalry, rode in advance of his regiment, and made good use of his sabre ...Private Douglass, company C, Fourth United States cavalry, rode by the side of Captain McIntyre, and brought in fifteen prisoners, three of them being commissioned officers.

Private William Bailey, Fourth Michigan Cavalry, specially distinguished himself by riding through a narrow gap in the fence in front of the enemy's artillery, galloping into the battery, and shooting the captain dead on the spot. I beg most respectfully to call the attention of the general to these gallant private soldiers.

The following list of casualties is officially reported, but should be corrected to the extent of placing most of the "missing" in the column of killed or wounded:

FIRST BRIGADE.

REGIMENTS.	KILLED.		WOUNDED.		MISSING.		TOTAL.	
	Officers.	Men.	Officers.	Men.	Officers.	Men.	Officers.	Men.
Fourth United States, .	.....	10	1	10	1	20	2	40
Seventh Pennsylvania,	.....	5	....	12	3	24	3	41
Fourth Michigan, ...	.....	2	1	6	....	9	1	17
Head-quarters, ...	.....	....	....	1	1	.....	1	1
Total in brigade, ...	.....	17	2	29	5	53	7	99
Second Brigade.								
First Ohio,...........	.....	4	....	13	....	2	....	19
Third Ohio, ...	1	7	....	30	....	7	1	44
Fourth Ohio,.........	.....	3	2	16	2	5	4	24
Head-quarters, ...	.....	....	2	.....	....	...	2	....
Board of Trade battery,	.....	1	....	4	.	1	....	6
Total aggregate, ...	1	32	6	92	7	68	14	192

Of the officers reported "missing," Lieutenant Heber S. Thompson, Seventh Pennsylvania, and brigade inspector First brigade, was wounded and captured.

Captain Percy H. White, Seventh Pennsylvania, was captured.

Captain James G. Taylor, Seventh Pennsylvania, was killed.

Lieutenant C. C. Hermans, Seventh Pennsylvania, was killed.

As this charge at Lovejoy covered a frontage of a line of battle over a mile in length, different eye-witnesses describe the affair with some considerable variations from the text, as well as from each other. The author describes it from his place in the ranks, to wit, the extreme front and right of the charging columns; correspondents to different newspapers stating what they saw on the left and centre. A correspondent of the Cincinnati Commercial says:

While the various regiments were being manoeuvred into position to meet the onslaught of the rebels, who were sweeping down upon them, the men had time to comprehend the danger that surrounded them—rebels to the right of them, rebels to the left of them, rebels in the rear of them, rebels in front of them—surrounded; there was no salvation but to cut their way out. Visions of Libby prison and starvation flitted through their imagination, and they saw that the deadly conflict could not be avoided. Placing himself at the head of his brigade, the gallant and fearless Minty drew his sabre, and his voice rang out clear and loud: "Attention, column! Forward, trot; regulate by the centre regiment; march, gallop, march!" and away the brigade went with a yell that echoed away across the valleys.

The ground from which the start was made, and over which they charged, was a plantation of about two square miles, thickly strewn with patches of woods, deep water cuts, fences, ditches," and morasses. At the word, away went the bold dragoons at the height of their speed. Fences were jumped and ditches were no impediment. The rattle of the sabres mingled with that of the mess-kettles and frying-pans that jingled at the side of the pack-mule brigade, which were madly pushed forward by the frightened darkies who straddled them.

Charging for their lives, and yelling like devils, Minty and his troopers encountered the rebels behind a hastily constructed barricade of rails. Pressing their rowels deep into their horses' flanks, and raising their sabres aloft, on, on, on, nearer and nearer to the rebels they plunged.

The terror-stricken enemy could not withstand the thunderous, wave of men and horses that threatened to engulf them. They broke and ran just as Minty and his troopers were urging their horses for the decisive blow. In an instant, all was confusion. The yells of the horsemen were drowned in the clashing of steel and the groans of the dying. On pressed Minty in pursuit, his men's sabres striking right and left, and cutting down everything in their path. The rebel horsemen were seen to reel and pitch headlong to the earth, while their frightened steeds rushed pell-mell over their bodies. Many of the rebels defended themselves with almost superhuman strength; yet it was all in vain. The charge of Federal steel was irresistible. The heads and limbs of some of the rebels were actually severed from their bodies, the head of the rider falling on one side of the horse, the lifeless trunk upon the other.

The individual instances of heroism were many. Hardly a man flinched, and when the brigade came out, more than half the sabres were stained with human blood.

It was, all admit, one of the finest charges of the war. Fully one hundred men fell under the keen sabres of Minty's brigade. The praises of Minty and his command are upon every tongue. The Fourth United States, Fourth Michigan, First, Third, and Fourth Ohio regiments charged over a rebel battery of three guns on the left of the road; but no sooner had our men passed than the rebels again seized the cannon, and reversing them, poured grape and canister into the charging columns. General Kilpatrick, seeing this, with his staff and others, about thirty in all, moved forward to capture the guns, but found a high staked-and-ridered fence between him and the battery.

Seeing the predicament in which the general was, Private William Bailey, a young Tennessean belonging to company I, Fourth Michigan, an orderly to Colonel Minty, coolly rode up to the fence, dismounted in the face of a severe fire, tore down the fence, remounted, rode up to the battery, shot the captain, took possession of the horse and arms, and rode out. He was immediately followed by a party of men, who captured the battery and spiked the guns. In the charge, Minty's brigade captured three stand of colours, the Fourth United States taking two, and the Fourth Michigan one.

The following is from a Michigan paper, but being an old clipping, the author is unable to give the proper credit:

With one division of infantry in front of us, and three brigades of cavalry in our rear, we could not entertain any very pleasant feelings, you may be assured. While thus situated, and each man meditating upon future life in some Southern prison, it was announced to us that General Kilpatrick was going to cut his way through the cavalry. Minty's brigade was mounted and ordered back in that direction, and while forming for the charge, the rebel infantry were held by Kilpatrick's division, under command of Colonel Murray, of the Third Kentucky cavalry. The brigade was formed on the right of the road, within gun-shot of the rebel line, but so quickly was it done that they did not divine the movement. And now comes one of the most brilliant sabre charges that has been made during this war, either in this department or elsewhere. It requires a more able pen than mine to give it a correct description.

The brigade was formed in three columns, the Fourth regulars on the left, the Seventh Pennsylvania on the right, and the Fourth Michigan in the centre. When everything was in readiness the general came up, drew his sabre, and took position at the head of the Fourth regulars. Colonel Minty was in front of the centre of his brigade, and when notified that everything was ready, gave the command to draw sabre. Every sabre leaped from its scabbard, and then came the clear ringing voice of our brave little colonel, "Forward! regulate to the centre regiment, charge!" The whole brigade moved as one man, yelling and shouting, the colonel all the time at the front leading them on. The enemy opened with grape and canister, and shell from their battery, and the dismounted cavalry poured in a volley from their guns, but it was but one volley only; before they could again load and fire, we were among them with our sabres, cutting them down on every side. The battery was silenced in no time, one gun being upset, while we took the other one along with us. In less time than it takes to relate it, we had run over and cut our way through three brigades of cavalry, and made a road for the remainder of the command to pass out, which it did with safety, artillery, ambulances, pack mules and all.

General Kilpatrick's headquarters flag was pierced by a shell in making a charge, and Colonel Minty's horse was slightly wounded by a musket ball from the line of the dismounted cavalry. Had we the time, we could have brought off five or six hundred prisoners, but they were in close pursuit, and we were obliged to leave them behind in order to secure our own safety. Our ambulances were loaded with wounded, the horses of the command very much fatigued, and our progress was occasionally very slow. We brought out about thirty prisoners only, and about one hundred horses and mules.

In going out the command had become somewhat confused and disorganised, and in order that we might the better be prepared for work, the general ordered a halt and reorganisation. When the reorganisation was about completed, the enemy overtook us and attacked Colonel Long with great fury, who again happened to be in the rear. It was all he could do to hold them until the column got straightened out on the road, but at the sacrifice of about fifty men he succeeded in holding them. The colonel himself was twice severely wounded in this engagement, and had to be carried from the field.

The Fourth Michigan and Seventh Pennsylvania were now dismounted and deployed across the road for the purpose of protecting the retreat of Colonel Long's brigade. We remained in line until the brigade had passed, followed by the rebels, but the reception with which they were met a few moments before prevented them from attacking us with the same impetuosity with which they had rushed on to Colonel Long's command. After skirmishing with them a short time, we withdrew and closed up with the column. That was the last time they bothered us on the march. Darkness now set in, and we marched until two o'clock, when we crossed a deep stream, burning the bridges after us, and went into camp until morning.

At sunrise, the column was again on the move, and after marching three miles we came to a stream which had been so swollen by recent rains that the whole command had to swim it. Three men and several animals were drowned, and one ambulance and two wagons lost in crossing. That night we went into camp in good season at Lithonia, a village on the Augusta railroad, about fifteen miles from the left of our army. Considering ourselves out of danger, we slept soundly, which was the first night's rest we had since leaving camp on the morning of the 18th.

"The next morning at sunrise we again resumed the march, and arrived inside our lines at an early hour in the afternoon, having been completely around the rebel army. Of one thing we were completely satisfied, that General Kilpatrick is entitled to the cognomen which was given him on the Potomac, *viz*.: of "Kill Cavalry." But of another thing we are satisfied, also, that he is one of the very best cavalry generals in the service. He knows exactly how to handle cavalry, is not afraid to fight, and is always at the front in person, willing to take his own chances with the rest.

The following extract from the Memphis-Atlanta Appeal, published in Macon, Georgia, in September, 1864, is given, showing the fact that Cleburne's infantry was cut to pieces, as stated in the text:

The newspapers have lately been full of accounts of how Martin's division of cavalry was 'run over' by the Yankees at Lovejoy, on the 20th *ult*. The writer was on the field on that occasion, and, in justice to the much-abused cavalry, states the facts in the matter: Martin's division, supporting the battery, was formed on the McDonough road. Ross' and Ferguson's commands, on foot, were in front and on each side of the battery, behind rail breast-works. A brigade of Cleburne's division was on the left of the road, in three lines, the last one in a piece of woods, about one hundred yards in rear of the position of the battery. On the right of the road (east side) the State troops were formed in line. When the Yankees charged, they came in a solid column, ten or twelve lines deep, running their horses, and yelling like devils. They didn't stop to fire or attempt to keep any kind of order or formation, but, each fellow for himself, rushed on, swinging his sabre over his head. They rode right over Ross' and Ferguson's men in the centres and over and through Cleburne's lines, one after the other, on the left. Cleburne's first line, they say, tried to use their bayonets, but the Yankees cut them to pieces.

After the Yankees had cut through all the other forces and captured the battery, Martin, seeing the field was lost, retreated in good order to the east and joined Cleburne's main body, and aided in the final defeat of the enemy on the McDonough road that evening, and pursued them to and through McDonough that night, recapturing nearly five hundred of our men, which they took in the charge. The effort to arouse the people against

Martin and his brave division is more disgraceful and demoralising than the Yankees' 'charge' itself, and should be frowned upon by all who wish well to our cause.

The following account of the "Kilpatrick raid" is taken from a private letter, written by Captain Robert Burns, acting assistant adjutant general of the First brigade, and is inserted as written to give the reader an idea of how the men felt, and how they described to their friends at home the stirring scenes through which they passed:

Headquarters First Brigade Second Cavalry Division,
Near Sandtown, G-a., August 28, 1864.
My Dear D——: A few days ago I wrote you a few lines announcing my sale return from one of those raids, which have generally been so unfortunate in this department. On the 18th, at 1 a. m., ours, and Colonel Long's brigade, the First and Second, all under Colonel Minty, left our Peach Tree Creek camp, on the left of our army, and at seven the next morning reported to General Kilpatrick at Sandtown, having, during the night, passed in the rear of our army to its right. We remained quietly at Sandtown during the 19th, and at sundown started to cut the rebel communications south of Atlanta. Two well equipped expeditions, Stoneman's and McCook's, had been totally ruined in attempting the same thing. We, however, imagined we were made of sterner stuff, and started off in good spirits.

The command consisted of the Third cavalry division (Kilpatrick's), under Colonel Murray, of the Third Kentucky cavalry, being Fifth Iowa, Third Indiana, Eighth Indiana, Second Kentucky, Third Kentucky, Fifth Kentucky, Tenth Ohio, and Ninety-Second Illinois, about 2,700 men, and our brigade, the Fourth United States, Seventh Pennsylvania, and Fourth Michigan, and Colonel Long's, the First Ohio, Third Ohio, and Fourth Ohio, the two latter brigades being under the command of Colonel Minty.

We knew that all the fighting would have to be done by us and Long's men before we started, and so it turned out. We had about 2,700 men with us, too. The whole was commanded by General Kilpatrick, and a good deal of a little man he is, too; not at all afraid to be in the fight himself. Away we went. Colonel Murray's division being in the advance. It was a bright, beautiful moonlight night, and we should have enjoyed it more if we had not been up all the night preceding. We had not gone more than three miles when we ran into the enemy's pickets. Then we had to go slowly, driving them before us, dismounting to feel the woods on both sides, &c., so that it was morning before we reached the Atlanta and West Point railroad, near Fairburn, at Red Oak. We had torn up about half a mile of track, and were moving on, when the rear battalion of the Seventh Pennsylvania was suddenly attacked by a force of dismounted men and artillery. (The column, you must know, was four or five miles long, and the rear or front might be fighting briskly and the other eiid know nothing about it, except when the artillery was opened.)

Just back of where the rebels struck our column were the ambulances, and the darkies leading officers, horses, pack-mules, &c. They, of course, skedaddled, each nigger and ambulance-driver bolted for the woods. Several shells exploded among the coloured brethren, and they thought the kingdom had come. Three ambulances were smashed to pieces, and about fifty of the sneaks who hang around the doctors' shops were scattered into the woods. I thought my lead horse was gone, but finally my contraband came crawling out of the woods, soared almost white. The Fourth Michigan, which was in the rear of the ambulances, soon came up, and drove the rebels back to their haunts. All this time the head of the column was kept moving on, as time was precious, and we could not halt for slight "scrimmages."

General Kilpatrick, not being satisfied with the progress Colonel Murray was making, ordered our brigades to come to the front, and Murray to take the rear. Long's brigade had the advance, and had not gone more than half a mile, when he found a strong force of rebs in his front. He had to dismount Ms men, drive them from the rail breast-works they had thrown up, mount again, and he would find them in the same position a half mile farther on. This was tried two or three times, when it was determined to march on foot altogether, and drive the rebels steadily, having men behind to lead the horses, from which the riders had dismounted.

I was up at the front all the time with Colonels Long and Minty. We drove them steadily until we came to the valley through which Flint River runs, when the rebels were reinforced by

Ferguson's brigade of cavalry (we had been fighting Ross' brigade thus far), and opened on us sharply with artillery, when we commenced descending the hill. The shells and bullets rattled merrily around us, knocking the bark and dirt in close proximity to our heads. Two guns of our battery (we had with us four guns of the Chicago Board of Trade Battery, which belongs to our division, and Murray had with him four guns of the Eleventh Wisconsin battery) were soon brought up, and succeeded in silencing the rebel artillery. The very first shot struck a rebel artilleryman, burst in him, and blew him to atoms.

Our men were all then dismounted, and went forward at the double quick, under fire of our eight guns, and drove the rebels clear into and through Jonesboro'. Our regiment had the advance, being deployed as skirmishers. We then seized the railroad, for which we had been aiming since we started, and commenced to smash it generally. The track was torn up, the depot and public buildings burned, and destruction was let loose. We destroyed about two miles of the track. While this was going on, the rebels returned to the attack. Our command was sent to meet them, while Colonel Murray's turned over rails.

The rebs had been driven southward, and our forces were pushed that way to shove them farther. Before us was darkness and rebels; behind, the burning buildings and smoking ruins. It also commenced to thunder, lighten and pour down rain. All this time, while we were skirmishing with the rebels, General Kilpatrick had one of his bands close behind us playing *Yankee Doodle, Hail Columbia*, and other airs, very provoking to rebel ears.

It appeared as if chaos had come again. Soon the whistle of the cars could be heard in front of us, and we knew by the sounds that the enemy were receiving reinforcements from below. It was then determined to "flank" them. So, about midnight, our brigade, followed by Colonel Murray's division, moved in a south-easterly direction, about seven miles. Colonel Long's brigade being left to cover the rear. I stayed with Colonel Long's command. While waiting for the command to move out, I fell asleep on the ground, and came very near being left. However, we all got away clear.

About seven miles out we found our brigade and Colonel Murray's command feeding by the side of the road. Our brigade was on a hill about a mile in front of Colonel Murray. Both hills were cleared, and the valley had but few trees in it. I rode over to our brigade and sat down to get a bite. Colonel Long halted just in rear of Colonel Murray. (This was about 6 a.m., on the 20th.) Our, brigade had just been ordered to mount and move forward, when Colonel Long was attacked by the rebel cavalry, which had followed us from Jonesboro'. It now consisted of Ross', Ferguson's, and Armstrong's brigades, about 4,500 men. Our brigade moved on and turned sharply to the right, in a south-westerly direction, for the purpose of striking the railroad again, about eight miles below Jonesboro'. I stayed on the hill to witness the skirmishing for a little while. From where I was all the manoeuvres of our men could be distinctly seen. It was a beautiful sight. The rebels could be perceived moving towards our men, and were driven back whenever seen by them. It was the best chance I ever had of seeing the whole of a skirmish. I remained as long as I could, and then galloped after our column.

Colonel Long had orders to follow as quickly as possible, and Colonel Murray was to come after him. We, in the meantime, pushed for Lovejoy's station. When within a mile and a half of the railroad, we halted for Colonels Murray and Long to join us. This they soon did, having driven back the enemy. About a mile from the railroad, the road forked, the two prongs striking it about a half a mile apart. A few hundred feet in front of, and parallel to, the railroad, another road ran.

The Fourth Michigan was sent by the right hand road to the railroad, which it reached without any difficulty, and commenced tearing up the track. They sent word to us by the parallel road, mentioning what they were doing. Our column, the Seventh Pennsylvania, in advance, moved down the left hand road, having for the last mile or two been driving about a dozen rebel cavalrymen. As we passed the parallel road, the firing became hotter and heavier.

I had been with the advance urging them forward, as it was extremely necessary to reach the railroad as soon as possible, and rode back to have more men sent to reinforce the advance guard, when a *devil* of a fusillade took place. The Seventh Pennsylvania was immediately dismounted, and sent forward into the woods. (One battalion of it had been the advance guard.)

Hotter grew the firing, and the horses of the advance, who had dismounted, began to hurry back. The Fourth regulars, who were next, were dismounted and sent in, and I was told to go back, and hurry up two of Long's regiments, have them dismount, and push in. Before that could be done, the Seventh Pennsylvania and Fourth Regulars had been driven from the woods in confusion, the former leaving two captains and one lieutenant, and the latter one captain, in the hands of the enemy, dead or wounded.

We had run on a brigade of rebel infantry who were lying in the woods, by the side of the railroad, behind barricades. A division was also pushing in on our right, near the point where the Fourth Michigan were at work.

Long's men were immediately put in position to check the advancing rebels, and our battery brought up. The woods in front and on our left, were swarming with rebels. The Fourth Regulars and Seventh Pennsylvania were gathered together and made to support the battery. Poor fellows, they were badly cut up. One of Long's regiments was formed near the fork of the road, the Fourth Michigan was sent for, and placed there too. The rebels tried again and again to take our battery. It fought magnificently. It was a glorious sight to see it sweep those woods with grape and canister, sending many a howling rebel into eternity.

The guns were made to radiate in all directions, and did work splendidly. Our men supported them well. One of the guns, by the rebound, had broken its trail short off, so that it could not be drawn from the field. When the rest of the pieces had been withdrawn, Colonel Minty called for some volunteers to drag off that gun by hand. I collected about twenty of the Fourth Michigan men, went down there, and helped pull it off. The rebels were then very close to us. While this was going on, we could hear musketry and artillery firing directly in our rear. The cavalry, with which we had been skirmishing early in the morning, had followed us, and had attacked us from "behind."

Thus, you see, we were in a pretty tight box: A brigade of infantry in our front, and partly on our left; a division moving to hit us on the right, and but a little distance off; and three brigades of cavalry in our rear. Stoneman and McCook caved in under just such circumstances. It was quickly decided what to do. We must leave the railroad alone for the present, and smash the rebel cavalry. We were withdrawn from fighting the infantry, who now had become very quiet, probably because effecting some combinations with their cavalry, and expecting confidently to "gobble" us all.

The whole command was faced to the rear, as follows: Our brigade was formed on the right hand side of the road, each regiment in a column of fours, *i.e.*, four men abreast, or the whole regiment in a column, presenting a front of only four men. The Fourth United States were on the left, the Fourth Michigan in the centre, and Seventh Pennsylvania on the right. Long's brigade formed in close column, with regimental front, *i.e.,* each regiment formed in line, the men side by side thus:

	Fourth *United States.*	*Fourth* *Michigan.*	*Seventh* *Pennsylvania.*
	││││	││││	││││
	││││	││││	││││
	││││	││││	││││
	││││	││││	││││
	││││	││││	││││
	││││	││││	││││
		││││	││││
First Ohio,	││││││││││││││││││		
Third Ohio,	││││││││││││││││││││		
Fourth Ohio,	││││││││││││		

The last regiment was deployed in rear of the others, so as to cover a large space of ground, and pick up prisoners and trophies. You see, we were to break through the rebels and smash them, and Long was to sweep the ground and gather them in. This was very quickly determined and acted on, as we had not much time to lose.

I happened to be near General Kilpatrick before he determined what to do. One brigade was then drawn up in line, in front of the Second brigade. He turned to me and asked, "Captain, can your men charge through and break those rebels in front of us?"

"Yes, sir, they can."

"What would be the best formation, do you think? In line, or in column?"

"In columns of four, I think, each regiment to form a column, and then the rebels' attention would be distracted."

" We will have them so. How do they generally charge—with sabre or firing?"

"With sabre, sir."

"Good! Go tell Colonel Minty to have them charge in that way, and drive the —— rebels —— to ——."

At this moment Colonel Minty rode up, and the regiments were quickly formed as I have marked.

A few of our men were in front of us dismounted, skirmishing with the rebels. They were told to throw down the fence behind which they were. The rebel skirmishers were keeping them engaged as much as possible, while a large force of them were throwing up rail breastworks. We were formed just behind the brow of a hill. Our skirmishers were on the crest of it. The rebel artillery to our left and front was playing over us. Bullets and shot were flying thick over our heads. We drew sabres, trotted until we came to the hill, and then, with cheer upon cheer, started at the gallop. What a sight it was! I rode at the head of the Fourth Michigan, or centre column, Captain Thompson, our inspector, on my right, and Colonel Minty on the right of Thompson.

Down the hill we went, the rebels turning their batteries of grape and canister upon us, while the bullets of the skirmishers and dismounted men whistled freely. The battery away on our right threw shells. We leaped fences, ditches, and barricades, and were among them. Their skirmish line did not attempt to stand, and the men behind the barricades turned to run just before we reached them. It was too late. Our fellows were mounted and on the gallop, and we did cut them down right and left. I was just about to strike two. when they threw up their hands and surrendered. I passed them by, leaving someone in the rear to take care of them.

A third, who did not surrender quick enough, I struck full on the top of the head, felt my sabre sink in, saw him fall, and dashed on. I think I killed him, but did not wait to see. The rebel artillery was very hot at this time. I could almost feel the balls as they swept by. Colonel Minty's horse was shot. Poor Thompson was hit close by my side, and fell. He is yet missing, and we do not know what has become of him. The last seen of him he was dismounted, wounded, and trying to rally some men to take the rebel battery. I hope he is not dead. Our column and the Seventh Pennsylvania dashed straight forward into the woods. The field over which we passed was at least a halt a mile wide, with three fences, one partially built barricade, and a half dozen ditches or gullies, washed out by the rain, from two to six feet deep, and from five to thirteen feet wide. We would no sooner leap one of them when we would have to go flying over another.

Our horses went kiting over the fences, some of them they knocked down. Of course, a good many of our men were dismounted. Upon reaching the woods we could not go fast, and could not keep in column. They were full of flying rebels. We soon struck a path or lane, and turning to the right, followed it about a mile and a half, when we turned to the left and joined the main column on the road. The Fourth regulars, instead of keeping parallel with us, as was intended, seeing an opening in the fence by the side of the road, and finding very high fences in front of them, turned to the left and struck out on the main road. They ran on the rebels in the road near the battery, and sent them flying, and were soon among the led horses of the dismounted men in the rear, and among the ambulances, which were collected together in a disorganised body in the road.

A perfect stampede took place. The horse-holders did not attempt to hold the animals, and a general "skedaddle" took place. Riderless horses and driverless ambulances were scattered in all directions. Our men were in the midst of them, shooting and cutting. As the rear of the Fourth regulars was passing the battery, a part of them, with scattered men from other regiments, dashed on to it, drove the gunners from their pieces, and captured three of the guns. One of our orderlies shot the captain. We brought away the pieces with us. The other two were so injured about their running gear that they could not be hauled off, so they were spiked and left.

The charge continued for about two miles, when the command was collected together again. Colonel Long's brigade did not charge in line, as it was intended, but finding the ground impracticable for it, formed in column and followed the Fourth Regulars. Colonel Murray's command, instead of sweeping all to the left of the road, as we supposed they would do, turned to the right, and filed in after Colonel Long. Had he (Murray) done as was expected, both sides of the road would have been cleaned out. As it was, a good many of the rebels escaped off to the left.

Immediately after the charge, and while we were pushing through the woods, it commenced to rain. It came down in torrents. I had lost both hat and rubber overcoat in the brush, and in just five seconds was soaked, saturated, even my boots were so filled that the water ran out of the tops. The command was gathered together about two or three miles from where we started, and pushed on for McDonough. Before the whole of it had moved off, Colonel Long's brigade, which had been moved to cover the rear, was fiercely attacked by the division of rebel infantry, which I have mentioned, was moving in on our right, as we faced the railroad, our left and rear as we were now going. Colonel Long fought them for about two hours, when his ammunition began to give out. He was obliged to retire (here Colonel Long was wounded twice), and the Fourth Michigan and Seventh Pennsylvania were formed a short way behind him, behind rail breast-works, which they had been ordered to hastily throw up. The Fourth regulars had been sent on, their ammunition having been all expended. We borrowed one of Long's regiments to assist the Fourth Michigan and Seventh Pennsylvania.

Long passed his men through, when the rebels came on us. There we had it, hot and heavy. The rebels charged two or three times, but were bloodily repulsed. All this fighting was done dismounted, and was for the purpose of holding back the rebels until our main column could get out of the road. Our battery, of three guns now, during this fight, burst one gun, and wedged another (got a shell half way down in it, so that it could neither be fired nor pushed down), so that we had but one to use, but that was used with effect. The rebels were playing with their artillery into our column along the road. You see our two brigades had to do all the fighting, obliged to lead the charge, and cover the retreat.

As soon as all the column had got into the road, and moved about a mile, our regiments were withdrawn, and followed it. The rebels did not attempt to pursue much farther. Their infantry could not keep up with us, and their cavalry was too thoroughly scattered to be gathered together again. We pushed slowly on to McDonough, crossed Walnut Creek, and about two o'clock in the morning lay down by the side of the road for a few hours' rest. How terribly tired we were! Men would tumble from their horses, and it would be almost impossible to awaken them. Two or three men would fall asleep together upon their horses, their horses would stop, and the whole column behind them would stop, too, supposing that there were some obstructions ahead. Hundreds of men were sometimes asleep in that way on their horses, and in the mud, for two or three hours at a time.

Once during one of the halts, I fell asleep on my horse for two hours, during which time we had a terrible storm of rain, which drenched me more, if possible, than I was. I knew nothing of it until I awoke, and then found myself in a strange crowd, the column in the meantime having moved on. It was raining and pitch dark, and, in fine, we had a terribly disagreeable time of it. About two o'clock we found a place to halt. The head of the column had been in at eight, but the tail was delayed by the causes I have mentioned.

You never yet knew what fatigue is. We had not slept a wink, for the nights of 17th, 18th, 19th, and until two o'clock of the morning of the 21st, except what we could snatch riding along. We had not had but three meals, and but little time to eat them in. Had fought seven pretty tough fights, besides skirmishing, &c., &c. Oh! how tired and sleepy I was! At daybreak the next morning we started on again. At Cotton River the bridge was gone, and the stream terribly swollen by the rains. It could not be forded, and the horses were obliged to swim it. The current was very swift. We had a terrible time crossing it. One man and about fifty horses were drowned in the attempt. We were obliged to leave behind the disabled cannon we had brought thus far in a wagon.

A good many men who had gone through the fighting bravely dreaded to enter that stream. We lost also two wagons, and one ambulance. It was almost heart-rending to see the poor wounded fellows carried across. Some were fastened on horses, while others were carried over in the ambulances. I saw one, with three in, tip over, fill with water, and go down the stream. However, the men were rescued. I shall never forget crossing Cotton River. We all finally got over. If we had been attacked by a large force before we had succeeded in crossing, a great number of us would have been captured. We were almost wholly out of ammunition, and many an anxious glance was cast to the rear. We expected every moment to hear the roar of artillery. It was a relief when the rear of the column was on the north side. We then crossed South River, burning the bridge behind us, and all the bridges on each side for ten miles.

During the day, we marched slowly, and encamped that night at Lithonia. The next day we returned to our camp on Peach Tree Creek, having made a circuit around the two great armies of Hood and Sherman. We did not do all that we had hoped to do when we started, but we did all we could.

Lieutenant S. B. Barron
Third Texas Cavalry
Photo 1882

Kilpatrick's Raid

By S. B. Barron

On the night of August 18, Ross' brigade was bivouacked a short distance east of the road leading from Sand Town, on the Chatta-hoochee River, to Fairburn, on the West Point Railroad, eighteen miles west of Atlanta, thence to Jonesboro, on the Macon Railroad, some twenty miles south of Atlanta. This latter was the only railroad we then had which was of any material value to us, and we knew that General Sherman was anxious to destroy it, as an unsuccessful effort in that direction had been made only a few days previous.

We had a strong picket on the Sand Town and Fairburn road, and, as all was quiet in front, we "*laid us down to sleep,*" and, perchance, to dream—of home, of the independence of the Confederate States, and all that was most dear to us. It was one of those times of fair promises, to the weary soldier, of a solid night's rest, so often and so rudely broken. Scarcely had we straightened out our weary limbs and folded our arms to sleep, when we were aroused by the shrill notes of the bugle sounding "boots and saddles." Our pickets were being driven in rapidly, and before we were in our saddles General Judson Kilpatrick, with a force of five thousand cavalry, with artillery, ambulances, pack mules and all else that goes to constitute a first-class cavalry raiding force, had passed our flank and was moving steadily down the Fairburn road. The Third Texas were directed to move out first and gain their front, to be followed by the other regiments of the brigade.

For the remainder of the night we moved as best we could down such roads as we could find parallel to Kilpatrick's line of march—so near, in fact, that we could distinctly hear the clatter of their horses' hoofs, the rumbling of their artillery, and the familiar rattle of sabres and canteens. Soon after daylight we came in sight of his column cross-ing the railroad at Fairburn, charged into it and cut it in two for the time. They halted, formed a line of battle, and we detained them in skirmishing until we managed to effect our object,—the gaining their front,—and during the day, until late in the afternoon, detained them as much as possible on their march.

Below Fairburn Kilpatrick's main column took the Jonesboro road, while a small column took the road leading to Fayetteville, a town about ten miles west of Jonesboro. Ross' brigade, continuing in front of the main column and that of Armstrong, followed the Fayetteville road. Just before night we passed through Jonesboro, which is ten or twelve miles from Fairburn, and allowed Kilpatrick to occupy the town for the night. Ross' brigade occupied a position south of the town near the railroad, while Armstrong was west; General Ferguson, whose brigade was numerically stronger than either of the others, being directed to go out on a road leading east. As we afterwards learned, they failed to find their road, or got lost, and, so far as I remember, were not heard from for a day or two. Thus posted, or intended to be posted, the understanding and agreement was that we should make a triangular attack on Kilpatrick at daylight the next morning.

Our brigade moved on time and marched into the town, only to learn that, with the exception of a few stragglers who had overslept themselves, not a Federal soldier was to be found. The brigade followed them eastwardly from Jonesboro, and in due time came up with their rear-guard at breakfast behind some railworks near Lee's Mill, and from this time until along in the afternoon we had a pretty warm time with their rear. They were moving on a road that intersects the McDonough and Love joy road, and when they struck this road they turned in the direction of Lovejoy Station.

We finally came up with the main force ensconced behind some heavy railworks on a hill near a farmhouse a short distance east of the station. We had to approach them, after leaving the timber, through a lane probably three-quarters of a mile in length. The farm was mostly uncultivated, and had been divided into three fields by two cross-fences, built of rails running at right angles with the lane, and these were thrown right and left to admit of the free passage of cavalry. In the eastern cross fence, however, a length some twenty or thirty yards, and but a few rails high, was left standing, when a ditch or ravine running along on the west side was too deep to be safely crossed by cavalry. In this lane the command dismounted, leaving the horses in the hands of holders, and deployed in line in the open field, to the left or south side of the lane, and a section of Croft's Georgia battery was placed on an elevation to the right of the lane.

I had been sent back to Lee's Mill to hurry up a detail left to bury one of our dead, so was behind when the line was formed. Having, on the day we fought McCook, picked up a mule for my boy Jake to ride, I now had him leading my horse to rest his back, while I rode the mule. I rode up and gave my rein to a horse-holder, and was hurrying on to join the line when they charged the railworks, and when I got up with them they had begun to fall back. The brigade, not having more than four hundred men for duty, was little more than a skirmish line. During the day General Hood had managed to place General Reynolds' Arkansas brigade at Lovejoy Station, which fact Kilpatrick had discovered, and while we were showing our weakness in an open field on one side, General Reynolds managed to keep his men under cover of timber on the other.

Thus Kilpatrick found himself between an unknown infantry force in front and a skirmish-line of dismounted cavalry and a section of artillery in his rear. He concluded to get out of this situation—and he succeeded. Being repulsed in the charge on the railworks, by a heavy fire of artillery and small arms, we fell back and re-formed our line behind the first cross fence. Three regiments of the enemy then rapidly moved out from behind their works, the Fourth United States, Fourth Michigan, and Seventh Pennsylvania, and charged with sabres, in columns of fours, the three columns abreast. As they came on us at a sweeping gallop, with their bright sabres glittering, it was a grand display. And Ross' brigade was there and then literally run over, trampled underfoot, and, apparently annihilated.

Just before the charge they had shelled our horses in the lane, which, consequently, had been moved back into the timber. What could we do under the circumstances? If we had had time to hold a council of war and had deliberated over the matter ever so long, we would probably have acted just as we did; that is, acted upon the instinct of self-preservation, rather than upon judgment. No order was heard; not a word spoken; every officer and every man took in the whole situation at a glance: no one asked or gave advice: no one waited for orders. The line was maintained intact for a few seconds, the men emptying their pieces at the heads of the columns. This created a momentary flutter without checking their speed, and on they came in fine style. There was no time for reloading, and every one instinctively started for the horses a mile in the rear, a half mile of open field behind us, and all of us much fatigued with the active duties performed on the sultry summer day.

Being very much fatigued myself and never being fleet of foot, I outran only two men in the brigade, Lieutenant W. H. Carr, of Company C, and W. S. Coleman, of Company A, of the Third Texas, who were both captured, and I kept up with only two others, Captain Noble and Lieutenant Soap, also of the Third Texas. We three came to the ravine already described, at the same instant. Soap dropped into it, Noble jumped over and squatted in the sage grass in the corner of the fence. I instantly leaped the ravine and the rail fence, and had gone perhaps ten or fifteen steps when the clatter of horses' hoofs became painfully distinct, and "Surrender, sir!" rang in my ear like thunder.

Now, I had had no thought of the necessity of surrendering, as I had fondly hoped and believed I would escape. Halting, I looked up to ascertain whether these words were addressed to me, and instantly discovered that the column directly in my wake was dividing, two and two, to cross the ravine, coming together again just in front of me, so that I was completely surrounded. This was an emergency. As I looked up my eyes met those of a stalwart rider as he stood up in his stirrups, his drawn sabre glittering just over my head; and, as I hesitated, he added in a kind tone: "That's all I ask of you, sir." I had a rifle in my hand which had belonged to one of our men who had been killed near me during the day. Without speaking a word, I dropped this on the ground in token of my assent. "All right," said he, as he spurred his horse to overtake some of the other men.

Just at this time our artillery began throwing shells across the charging columns, and the first one exploded immediately above our heads, the pieces falling promiscuously around in my neighbourhood, creating some consternation in their ranks. Taking advantage of this, I placed my left hand above my hip, as if struck, and fell as long a fall as I could towards the centre of the little space between the columns, imitating as best I could the action of a mortally wounded man,—carefully falling on my right side to hide my pistol, which I still had on. Here I lay, as dead to all outward appearances as any soldier that fell during the war, and remained in this position without moving a muscle, until the field was clear of all of Kilpatrick's men who were able to leave it.

To play the role of a dead man for a couple of hours and then make my escape may sound like a joke to the inexperienced, and it was really a practical joke on the raiders; but to me, to lie thus exposed on the bare ground, with a column of hostile cavalry passing on either side all the time, and so near me that I could distinctly hear any ordinary conversation, was far from enjoyable.

I am no stranger to the hardships of a soldier's life; I have endured the coldest weather with scant clothing, marched day after day and night after night without food or sleep; have been exposed to cold, hunger, inclement weather and fatigue until the power of endurance was well-nigh exhausted, but never did I find anything quite so tedious and trying as playing dead. I had no idea of time, except that I knew that I had not lain there all night. The first shell our men threw after I fell came near killing me, as a large piece ploughed up the ground near enough to my back to throw dirt all over me. Their ammunition, however, was soon exhausted, the guns abandoned, and that danger at an end.

As things grew more quiet the awful fear seized me that my ruse would be discovered and I be abused for my deception, and driven up and carried to prison. This fear haunted me until the last. Now, to add to the discomfort of my situation, it began to rain, and never in my life had I felt such a rain. When in my fall I struck the ground my hat had dropped off, and this terrible rain beat down in my face until the flesh was sore. But to move an arm or leg, or to turn my face over for protection was to give my case completely away, and involved, as I felt, the humiliation of a prison life; than which nothing in the bounds of probability in my life as a Confederate soldier was so horrible, in which there was but one grain of consolation, and that was that I would see my brother and other friends who had been on Johnson's Island for some months.

The last danger encountered was when some dismounted men came near driving some pack mules over me. Finally, everything became so quiet that I ventured to raise my head, very slowly and cautiously at first, and as not a man could be seen I finally rose to my feet. Walking up to a wounded Pennsylvania cavalryman I held a short conversation with him. Surveying the now deserted field, so lately the scene of such activity, and supposing as I did that Ross' brigade as an organisation was broken up and destroyed, I was much distressed. I was left alone and afoot, and never expected to see my horse or mule any more, which in fact I never did, as Kilpatrick's cavalry, after charging through the field, had turned into the road and stampeded our horses.

I now started out over the field in the hope of picking up enough plunder to fit myself for service in some portion of the army. In this I succeeded beyond my expectation, as I found a pretty good, completely rigged horse, only slightly wounded, and a pack-mule with pack intact, and I soon loaded the mule well with saddles, bridles, halters, blankets, and oil cloths. Among other things I picked up a Sharp's carbine, which I recognised as belonging to a messmate. While I was casting about in my mind as to what command I would join, I heard the brigade bugle sounding the assembly! Sweeter music never was heard by me. Mounting my newly-acquired horse and leading my pack-mule, I proceeded in the direction from which the bugle notes came, and on the highest elevation in the field, on the opposite side of the lane, I found General Ross and the bugler. I told my experience, and heard our gallant brigadier's laughable story of his escape. I sat on my new horse and looked over the field as the bugle continued to sound the assembly occasionally, and was rejoiced to see so many of our men straggling in from different directions, coming apparently out of the ground, some of them bringing up prisoners, one of whom was so drunk that he didn't know he was a prisoner until the next morning.

Near night we went into camp with the remnant collected, and the men continued coming in during the night and during all the next day. To say that we were crestfallen and heartily ashamed of being run over is to put it mildly; but we were not so badly damaged, after all. The horse-holders, when the horses stampeded, had turned as many as they could out of the road and saved them. But as for me, I had suffered almost a total loss, including the fine sword that John B. Long had presented me at Thompson's Station, and which I had tied on my saddle. My faithful Jake came in next morning, and although he could not save my horse, he had saved himself, his little McCook mule and some of my soldier clothes. My pack-mule and surplus rigging I now distributed among those who seemed to need them most.

Including officers, we had eighty-four or eighty-five men captured, and only sixteen or eighteen of these were carried to Northern prisons. Among them were seven officers, including my friend Captain Noble, who was carried to Johnson's Island, and messed with my brother until the close of the war. Captain Noble had an eye for resemblances. When he first saw my brother he walked up to him and said, "I never saw you before, but I will bet your name is Barron, and I know your brother well."

The other prisoners who escaped that night and returned to us next day included my friend Lieutenant Soap, who brought in a prisoner, and Luther Grimes, owner of the Sharp's carbine, already mentioned, who had an ugly sabre wound in the head. I remember only two men of the Third Texas who were killed during the day—William Kellum of Company C, near Lee's Mill; and John Hendricks, of Company B, in the charge on the railworks. These two men had managed to keep on details from one to two years, being brought to the front under orders to cut down all details to increase the fighting strength, and they were both killed on the field the first day they were under the enemy's fire.

Among the wounded was Captain S. S. Johnson, of Company K, Third Texas, gunshot wound, while a number of the men were pretty badly hacked with sabres. Next day General Ross went up to General Hood's headquarters and said to him: "General, I got my brigade run over yesterday."

General Hood replied, "General Ross, you have lost nothing by that, sir. If others who should have been there had been near enough to the enemy to be run over, your men would not have been run over."

This greatly relieved our feelings, and the matter became only an incident of the campaign, and on the 22nd day of August Ross' brigade was back in its position ready for duty.

UNION SOLDIER'S ACCOUNT OF KILPATRICK'S RAID

After the war ended I made a friend of Robert M. Wilson of Illinois, who served in the Fourth United States Cavalry, and he kindly wrote out and sent me his account of this raid, and by way of parenthesis I here insert it, as it may be of interest.

The following is an account of the Kilpatrick raid, made in August, 1864, written partly from memory and partly from a letter written August 28, 1864, by Captain Robert Burns, acting assistant adjutant-general of the First Brigade, Second Cavalry Division, I acting as orderly for him part of the time on the raid. I was detailed at brigade headquarters as a scout during the Atlanta campaign and until General Wilson took our regiment as his escort. On the 17th of August, 1864, at one o'clock, a. m., ours and Colonel Long's Brigade (the First and Second), of Second Cavalry Division, all under the command of Colonel Minty, left our camp on Peach Tree Creek, on the left of our army northeast of Atlanta, at seven o'clock next morning; reported to General Kilpatrick at Sand Town on the right of our army, having during the night passed from one end or flank of our army to the other.

We remained at Sand Town until sundown of the 18th, when we started out to cut the enemy's communications south of Atlanta. Two other expeditions, Stoneman's and McCook's, well equipped, before this had been ruined in attempting the same thing. We, however, imagined we were made of sterner stuff, and started off in good spirits. The command consisted of Third Cavalry Division (Kilpatrick's), under Colonel Murray, about 2700 men, and two brigades of our division (the Second), under command of Colonel Minty, about 2700 men also—the whole commanded by Kilpatrick (or Kill Cavalry, as we always called him).

Away we went, Third Division in advance. The night was a beautiful moonlight one, and we would have enjoyed it more if we had not been up all the night preceding. We did not go more than three miles before we ran into the enemy's pickets, when we had to go more slowly, driving them before us, dismounting to feel the woods on both sides, etc., etc. Consequently, it was morning when we reached the Atlanta & West Point Railroad near Fairburn. At Red Oak we had torn up about half a mile of the track when the rear battalion of Seventh Pennsylvania Cavalry was suddenly attacked by a force of dismounted men and artillery. Just back of where our column was struck were the ambulances, the darkies leading officers' horses, pack-mules, etc., etc. Several shells dropped among them, and they thought the kingdom had come, sure. The Fourth United States Cavalry, being in rear of the ambulances, soon drove the enemy away. All this time the head of the column kept moving on, as time was precious and we could not stop for slight scrimmages.

General Kilpatrick, not being satisfied with the progress made by his advance, ordered our brigades to take the front and Murray the rear. (We had learned before starting that it was expected we, our division, would do all the fighting.) Long's brigade, in advance, had not gone more than half a mile when he found a strong force of the enemy in his front. He had to dismount his men to drive the enemy from the rail barricades they had made, but he would find them in the same position half a mile farther on. Long kept his men dismounted, having number four lead the horses. I was close up with the advance with Colonel Minty. We drove the enemy steadily but slowly back, until we came to the valley through which Flint River runs, when they were re-inforced by Ferguson's brigade of cavalry (we had been fighting Ross' brigade thus far), and opened on us sharply with artillery when we commenced descending the hill, the shells and bullets rattling lively around us.

Two guns of our battery—we had with us four guns of Chicago Board of Trade which belonged to our division, and Murray had with him four guns of the Eleventh Wisconsin Battery—were soon brought up and succeeded in silencing the enemy's artillery, the first striking an artilleryman and blowing him to pieces. Our division were then all dismounted and moved forward at the double-quick under fire of our eight guns, and drove the enemy clear through Jonesboro, crossing the bridge on the stringer. Our brigade (First) had the advance, being nearly all deployed as skirmishers.

We then seized the railroad for which we had started, and we commenced to smash things generally. The track was torn up for about two miles, the depot and public buildings burned, and destruction was let loose. While this was going on the enemy returned to the attack, and our division was sent to meet them, the Third Division turning the rails. The enemy were driven southward and we were pushed that way, to shove them farther back. Before was darkness and death, behind the burning buildings and smoking ruins, and now it also began to thunder, lightning, and pour down rain in torrents.

All this time General Kilpatrick had one of his bands behind us playing *Yankee Doodle* and other patriotic airs. It appeared as if defeat was coming, for we could hear the whistle of the cars in front of us and knew that the enemy were being reinforced from below. We then determined to flank them, so about midnight our brigade, followed by the Third Division, moved in a southeasterly direction about seven miles, Long's brigade being left to cover the rear.

When seven miles out we stopped to feed, close to 6 a. m., about a mile from Murray's Division, but were little protected, as both hills were cleared and the valley had but few trees in it. Our brigade was ordered to mount and move forward when Colonel Long's brigade was attacked by the cavalry that followed us from Jonesboro. The enemy's forces consisted of the brigades of Ross, Ferguson, and Armstrong, about 4500 men. Our brigade moved on and turned sharply to the right, in a southwesterly direction, to strike the railroad again about eight miles below Jonesboro. I stayed on the hill with Captain Burns, for a short time, to witness the skirmishing between Long and the enemy. From where we were all our manoeuvres could be distinctly seen, as also the enemy, who would advance upon our men, only to be driven back. It was a beautiful sight. 'By Heaven, it was a noble sight to see—by one who had no friend or brother there.'

Captain Burns, myself following, now galloped off to overtake our brigade, which we soon did. Colonel Long had orders to follow as quickly as possible, Colonel Murray to come after. We (our brigade) pushed for Lovejoy Station. When within a mile and a half of the railroad we halted for the rest of the command to join us. About a mile from the railroad the road forks, the two prongs striking the railroad about a half a mile apart. A few hundred feet in front of and parallel to the railroad another road ran. The Fourth Michigan was sent by the right-hand road to the railroad, which it reached without any trouble; the rest of the brigade took the left-hand prong of the road, having for the last mile or two been driving off about a dozen cavalrymen. As we neared the railroad the firing became hotter and hotter.

The Seventh Pennsylvania Cavalry was dismounted and sent forward to the woods—one battalion, four companies, of it had been advance guard. Hotter grew the firing, and the horses of the advance who had dismounted came hurrying back.

The Fourth United States (Regulars) were then dismounted and sent in. Captain Burns was sent back to hurry up two of Long's regiments, but before this could be done the Seventh Pennsylvania and Fourth Regulars were driven from the woods in some confusion. We had run on a brigade of infantry who were lying in the woods behind barricades at the side of the rail-road, and a force of the enemy was also pushed in on the right, where the Fourth Michigan were at work. Long's brigade was put in position to check the advancing Confederates, and our battery brought up, as the woods in front and on our left were swarming with the enemy, and the Fourth Regulars and Seventh Pennsylvania were placed in support of the battery. Poor fellows, they were badly cut up!

One of Long's regiments was formed near the fork of the road, the Fourth Michigan was being placed there, and the enemy tried again and again to take our battery. It fought magnificently, and the guns were made to radiate in all directions and did splendid work, our men supporting them well. One of the guns, by the rebound, had broken its trail off short, so that it could not be drawn from the field. When the rest of the pieces had been withdrawn Colonel Minty called for men to draw off the piece by hand. Captain Burns took about twenty men of the Fourth Michigan Cavalry down and helped pull it off, though the enemy were very close to us. While this was taking place, heavy firing was heard in our rear, for the cavalry with which we had been fighting had followed us, and had us in a pretty tight box, as follows: a brigade of infantry in our front and partly on our left; a division moving on our right and but a short distance off; three brigades of cavalry in our rear. Stoneman and McCook threw up the sponge under like circumstances. We decided we must leave the railroad alone, and crush the enemy's cavalry, and consequently withdrew from fighting the infantry, who now became very quiet, probably expecting to soon take us all in.

The command was faced to the rear as follows: Our brigade was formed on the right hand side of the road, each regiment in columns of fours (four men abreast); the Fourth Regulars on the left; Fourth Michigan centre; Seventh Pennsylvania on the right, Long's brigade formed in close columns with regimental front, that is, each regiment formed in line, the men side by side, boot to boot, thus:

MINTY'S BRIGADE

FOURTH U. S.	FOURTH MICH.	SEVENTH PENN.
0 0 0 0	0 0 0 0	0 0 0 0
0 0 0 0	0 0 0 0	0 0 0 0
0 0 0 0	0 0 0 0	0 0 0 0
0 0 0 0	0 0 0 0	0 0 0 0
0 0 0 0	0 0 0 0	0 0 0 0

LONG'S BRIGADE

FIRST OHIO

0 0 0 0 0 0 0 0 0 0 0 0 0 0 0 0 0 0

THIRD OHIO

0 0 0 0 0 0 0 0 0 0 0 0 0 0 0 0 0 0 0 0

FOURTH OHIO

0 0 0 0 0 0 0 0 0 0 0 0 0 0 0 0 0 0 0 0

The last regiment was deployed in rear of the others so as to take in a large space of ground and pick up prisoners and trophies. You see, we were to break through the enemy, smashing them, and Long was to sweep over the ground and pick them up. This was soon determined on, for there was no time to lose. A few of our men were in front of us, dismounted, skirmishing with the enemy, and they were told to throw down the fence where they were. The enemy all this time was keeping them engaged as much as possible, while a large force of them were building rail barricades. We were formed just below the brow of the hill, skirmishers on the crest of it, the enemy's artillery to our left and front playing over us, and bullets and shells flying thick over our heads. We drew sabre, trotted until we came to the crest of the hill and then started at a gallop. Down the hill we went, the enemy turning canister upon us, while the bullets whistled fiercely, and the battery away on our right threw shells. We leaped fences, ditches, barricades, and were among them, the artillery being very hot at this time.

You could almost feel the balls as they passed by. The Fourth Michigan and Seventh Pennsylvania went straight forward to the woods, the field over which they passed being at least a half a mile wide, with three fences, one partially built barricade, and a number of ditches and gullies, some very wide and deep. Of course many of the men were dismounted, and upon reaching the woods they (our men) could not move fast, and they turned to the right and joined the main column in the road about one and a half miles from the start. The Fourth Regulars (my regiment, as I joined it when the charge was ordered) could not keep parallel with the rest of the brigade on account of high fences in our front, and seeing an opening in the fence we turned to the left, and struck out on the main road, coming upon the enemy in the road near their battery, and sending them flying.

We were soon among the led horses of the dismounted men in their rear and among the ambulances, and a perfect stampede took place, riderless horses and ambulances being scattered in all directions, we in the midst of them, shooting and cutting madly. A part of our regiment, with some of the Fourth Michigan and Seventh Pennsylvania, dashed at the battery, drove the men from the pieces, and captured three of the guns. Private William Bailey, a young Tennessean from near McMinnville, who belonged to Fourth Michigan Cavalry (he was associated with me at headquarters as scout), shot the captain. We brought away the guns, and the charge continued for about two miles, when we halted for the command to close up. Colonel Long's brigade did not charge in line as it was intended, for, finding that the ground

166

was impracticable, it formed in column and followed the Fourth Regulars. Colonel Murray's command, instead of sweeping all to the left, as we supposed they would do, turned to the right and followed Long. Had Murray done what was expected, both sides of the road would have been cleaned out.

Immediately after the charge and while we were pushing through the woods it commenced to rain, and poured in torrents. The command was now started for McDonough, but before the whole of it had moved off, Long's brigade, which had been moved to cover the rear, was fiercely attacked by the infantry of the enemy. Colonel Long fought them for about two hours, when, his ammunition giving out, he was obliged to retire. (Here Long was wounded twice.) The Fourth Michigan and Seventh Pennsylvania were formed in the rear, Long behind rail barricades which had been hastily thrown up. The Fourth United States Regulars being out of ammunition were sent on to McDonough, where the Ninety-Second Illinois Mounted Infantry divided ammunition with some of us near this town. One of Long's regiments assisted the Fourth Michigan and Seventh Pennsylvania. Long passed his men through when the enemy came on us. Then we had it hot and heavy, the enemy charging several times, but were repulsed.

All this fighting here was done dismounted, and was for the purpose of holding back the enemy until our main column could get out of the way. Our battery (three pieces) during this fight burst one gun and wedged another, getting a shell part way down it, so it could not be moved either way, so we had one gun only, but that was used with effect, the enemy meanwhile playing their artillery into our columns all along the road. You see our two brigades had to do all the fighting, lead the charge, and cover the retreat. As soon as our men had passed on about a mile, our rear-guard followed, and we were not molested again. We pushed slowly on to McDonough, crossed Walnut Creek, and near morning lay down in the mud for sleep. How tired we were I cannot tell, and men would tumble prone from their horses, and it was next to impossible to awaken them.

Frequently two or three men would fall asleep upon their horses, who would stop, and the whole column behind them would naturally do the same, too, supposing that there was obstruction ahead. Hundreds of men were sometimes asleep in that way upon their horses in the mud for an hour or so at a time. During this time, I fell asleep for about two hours, and awoke drenched to the skin, for it was raining, and fearfully dark and very disagreeable. About two o'clock we found a place to stop. I never before that knew what fatigue meant, for I had not slept a wink for the nights of the 17th, 18th, 19th, and 20th until the morning (about 2 a.m.) of the 21st, except what I had when riding along. We had had but three meals, and but little time to eat them, had fought seven pretty hard fights, besides skirmishing, etc., etc. At daybreak the next morning we started on again. At Cotton River the bridge was gone, the stream much swollen by rain, so that it could not be forded and the horses were obliged to swim it.

As the current was very swift, we had a terrible time crossing it. We, our brigade, lost one man and about sixty horses drowned here, and nearly all our pack-mules also. We could not get the wagon with the two disabled guns across at all, and rumour said they were buried here, and the site marked as the graves of two soldiers of the Fourth United States Cavalry. It was terrible to see the poor wounded carried across, some fastened on horses, while others were taken over in ambulances.

We all finally got over, but if the enemy had pushed us here most of the command would have been captured. We were now nearly all out of am munition, and many an anxious glance I gave to the rear, it being a relief when all were over. We then crossed South River bridge, burning all the bridges for ten miles each side, and camped that night at Lithonia. The next day we returned to our camp at Peach Tree Creek, having made a complete circuit of the two armies of Hood and Sherman. We did not do all we hoped we could when we started, but *we did all we could*. Notwithstanding what we had suffered, General Sherman was much dissatisfied with us, expecting more from us than lay in our power (or his either) to accomplish.

In the above narrative I have drawn very largely from a letter written August 28, 1864, by Captain Burns (as stated before), printed in a work called *Minty and the Cavalry*, though about all I have written occurred under my own observation. We captured three stands of colours claimed to belong to the Third Texas Cavalry, Zachariah Rangers, and Benjamin's Infantry.

Our aggregate loss in First and Second Brigades, killed, wounded, and missing, was 14 officers, 192 men.

Robert M. Wilson,
Company M, Fourth United States Cavalry.

★★★★★★

If the Third Texas colours were captured by them, they were found in an ambulance, as we did not have the flag unfurled on this expedition.

It will be noted here that the aggregate loss of 206 men is only the loss of one division, not including Kilpatrick's Division and the two batteries.

★★★★★★